P9-EEU-800

GERTRUDE STEIN

A Study of the Short Fiction

Also available in Twayne's Studies in Short Fiction Series

Twayne publishes studies of all major short-story writers
worldwide. For a complete list, contact the Publisher directly.

Twayne's Studies in Short Fiction

Gary Scharnhorst and Eric Haralson,
General Editors

GERTRUDE STEIN
The Yale Collection of American Literature, Beinecke Rare Book and Manuscript Library.
© *The Estate of Gertrude Stein. Reproduced by permission.*

GERTRUDE STEIN

A Study of the Short Fiction

Linda S. Watts
University of Washington, Bothell

TWAYNE PUBLISHERS
New York

Twayne's Studies in Short Fiction, No. 77

Gertrude Stein: A Study of the Short Fiction
Linda S. Watts

Copyright © 1999 by Twayne Publishers

All rights reserved. No part of this book may be reproduced or transmitted in any form or by any means, electronic or mechanical, including photocopying, recording, or by any information storage and retrieval system, without permission in writing from the Publisher.

Twayne Publishers
1633 Broadway
New York, NY 10019

Library of Congress Cataloging-in-Publication Data
Watts, Linda S., 1960–
    Gertrude Stein : a study of the short fiction / Linda S. Watts.
        p.   cm. — (Twayne's studies in short fiction ; no. 77)
    Includes bibliographical references and index.
    ISBN 0-8057-1696-3 (alk. paper)
        1. Stein, Gertrude, 1874–1946—Fictional works.
2. Fiction—Technique.   3. Short story.   I. Title.   II. Series.
PS3537.T323 Z887   1999
813'.5221—dc21   99-043647

This paper meets the requirements of ANSI/NISO Z3948-1992 (Permanence of Paper).

10 9 8 7 6 5 4 3 2 1

Printed in the United States of America

ACC Library Services
Austin, Texas

For Matthew

Contents

Preface

As we travel through our lives, we may reach moments in which we labor under the impression we have mastered the practices of reading and writing, only to discover that impression to be an illusion. One of my favorite literary selections in this regard is a short story by Jorge Luis Borges, "The Book of Sand."[1] It is the tale of an individual who fancies himself terribly clever for having purchased a most curious volume (for which the story is named). He finds it a book like no other he has encountered. Its pages, though bearing numerals, are not ordered in a continuous numerical sequence. Once he looks at a page, he can never locate it again. No matter how he manipulates the book, he cannot find a first page or, for that matter, a last one. Therefore, while the external appearance of the book (cover, title, bindings) remains constant, its contents are nonetheless undergoing continual transformation and renewal.

The balance of the story details the central character's response to this highly unusual acquisition. At first, the book serves as a kind of greedy pleasure for its new owner. He finds himself doing little else but pouring over the book, trying to unfold its mysterious message. He even comes to refuse the company and conversation of the people in his life—rather like new E-mail users, chatting eternally on the computer. All he can do is delight in his discovery, with a vigor that nears obsession.

As time elapses, however, the character finds himself tormented by the book's unwieldiness and his failure to master it. He comes to wish himself rid of the book for the very reason he at first felt he must possess it—its shape-shifting, its elusiveness, its infinite form of statement. He finds himself terrorized by the idea that he can never know the book completely or solve it like a riddle. It is never done being written, so its reading can never be concluded.

Reading and writing about the work of Gertrude Stein offers something of the same challenge as "The Book of Sand" poses to its protagonist. In engaging Stein, we try out for ourselves the notion that one is never done reading and writing—this for the very simple reason that we are never done thinking, and thank goodness for that! Encountering Stein is a process that finds us reflecting on reading as a journey rather than an arrival at a fixed, knowable destination. Indeed, in many cases, it is a journey that does not even end with the conclusion of the text's reading. Years later, we may find ourselves still reopening "books of sand" to read, write, and think anew. It is here that I trust the analogy to the Borges story ends, I hasten to add. In reading Stein, we try to dwell in the stage of fascination with language, meaning, and identity that accompanies the Borges character's initial relationship to the book, stopping well short of the phase in the tale in which he locks himself in a room, ceases all social contact, and descends into madness—those elements make a marvelously evocative literary experience, but in real life they constitute something of a hardship. So, if you have ever found that your experience of reading or writing a text changed you in lasting ways, and if you have ever known the pleasure of returning to books again and again, we have something exciting in common. What follows are my attempts to read Stein's books of sand. My objective is not to arrest the metamorphosis of the text or its readers but rather to celebrate and intuit the extraordinary movement of both in turn. No single reading of a Stein composition could ever suffice, so we perform readings today in the full and thankful knowledge that tomorrow, like the protagonist in the Borges story, we will find a changed book and a transfigured vision.

Notes

1. Jorge Luis Borges, "The Book of Sand," in *Other Voices, Other Vistas: Short Stories from Africa, China, India, Japan, and Latin America* (New York: Mentor, 1992).

Acknowledgments

I wish to offer thanks to Michelle Bonnice, Harriet Chessman, Bruce Martin, Thom Swiss, Drake University Center for the Humanities, those who granted permissions, the staff of Cowles Library, and especially the Estate of Gertrude Stein and the Yale Collection of American Literature, Beinecke Rare Book and Manuscript Library.

"Gertrude Stein: A Radio Interview," and Gertrude Stein's "All of It" and "Why I Like Detective Stories" are reprinted by permission of the Gertrude Stein Estate and the Yale Collection of American Literature.

Albert Mobilio, "The Lost Generator: Gertrude Stein Builds a Better Reader" [© Albert Mobilio] is reprinted by permission of the author. The essay first appeared in the *Voice Literary Supplement* 69 (November 1988): 7–13.

The section on *The World Is Round* appeared in an earlier form as "Twice Upon a Time: Back Talk, Spinsters, and Re-Verse-als in Gertrude Stein's *The World Is Round* (1939)," and is reprinted by permission of the publisher. The essay first appeared in *Women and Language* 16, no. 1 (Spring 1993): 53–57. [© Women and Language, 1993].

Part 1

THE SHORT FICTION

How (Next) to Read Gertrude Stein

> Reading Stein involves an almost unconditional willingness to
> be surprised.
>
> —Nancy Gray, *Language Unbound*

There are telling ways in which the careers—public and private—of
Oscar Wilde and Gertrude Stein coincide. Both earned and cultivated
reputations as immodest and transgressive literary figures. Both
inscribed controversial narratives of desire. Known for their conversation, wit, and epigrams, both captured the popular imagination. For
these trespasses, each was caricatured and maligned as a champion and
victim of excess. Each was dismissed by some critics as counterfeit.
Each built a career largely without the support of the academy. Both
conducted lecture tours in the United States and published accounts of
those tours, nearly exactly 50 years apart. Each wrote stories for children. Both found their final resting place at Pere Lachaise Cemetery,
the French National Cemetery located in Paris. Both continue to shape
the way readers and writers today understand the relationship between
center and margin, mainstream and subculture, poetry and paradox, letters and life.

The parallels do not end there. As if uncertainty and inconsistency
were the fashion of the day, both Wilde and Stein cloaked themselves in
literary and social ambiguity. Oscar Wilde once stated that "The way of
paradoxes is the way of truth. To test Reality we must see it on the
tight-rope. When the Verities become acrobats we can judge them."[1]
Like Wilde's, Stein's life and career were replete with paradoxes. She
knew and lived the life of an outsider—woman, lesbian, Jew, literary
outlaw—although that life had its privileges, such as wealth. She spent
her career in an elaborate game of hide-and-seek, as she sought attention but tried to direct it to a carefully contrived persona. She wanted
fame, but not at the price of artistic freedom or even convenience. She
wanted celebrity but found herself perplexed when people were more
interested in her life than her work. She wanted readers, but her writing was unyielding in its refusal to accommodate them. She wanted to

3

be acclaimed as a great writer without being tainted by the smell of the museums. She wanted to change writing practices and conventions but adamantly denied that she was engaged in experimentation. She wanted to write the Great American Novel even after she had declared the novel a dead form. She wanted the reputation of Proust or Joyce without the tether of association with them or their work. She refused to be a wife but insisted on having one. She wanted to live in Paris but did not wish to be considered an expatriate. She constantly reused words, motifs, and images within and across works but insisted that there was no repetition in her writing. She wrote of historical figures such as the Wright Brothers and Ulysses S. Grant but placed them within the "continuous present" of her prose. She worked obsessively but craved leisure and ease. She had the friendship and admiration of countless established and emergent writers and artists, only to squabble with and dismiss almost all of them. She held back for her whole life a novel about a lesbian love triangle, but meanwhile her writings were filled with the language women speak to each other when calling love names. In short, she resists summary or paraphrase.

As with her life, so her work. Stein does not readily permit her texts to be consumed or contained through traditional practices of reading and explication. Over the years, many readers (and, in the case of some detractors who bypassed the reading of her texts, onlookers) have found this fact alone unpardonable. For others, it is this effrontery that will always keep us reading Stein. As Ellen Berry has aptly noted, it is the difference between feeling resentment or gratitude that Stein's texts, to borrow Berry's phrase, "leave something to be desired."[2] There is more than delicious irony to a literary life so lived and a career so forwarded. It is to that "something more" that many contemporary readers of Stein pledge themselves; it is to that "something more" this book turns its energies. How (next) shall we read Gertrude Stein?

In the past, a wide range of readers, professional and avocational, has sought to understand the distinctive compositions of Gertrude Stein. Her signature moves to deform and reform literary language have prompted some to pronounce Stein the originator of a strange, new tongue—Steinese. I have written elsewhere, as have many recent critics, about the reading history of Stein's work.[3] Critics Sandra Gilbert and Susan Gubar offer a concise statement of that critical history's contours:

> Steinese has variously been understood as an incantatory form of chanting, as automatic writing, as a poetic equivalent to Cubist paint-

ing, as a literary analogue to atonal music, and as a linguistic form of either scientific relativism or philosophic nominalism. Most recently, the incomprehensibility of this writing has been explained in terms of two, quite different strategies. Some critics suggest that Stein's obfuscation is a camouflage to hide and simultaneously express her lesbianism in a hostile, heterosexual culture while others argue that it is a subversive strategy of deconstruction which critiques the phallogocentrism of language.[4]

While this passage provides a sound encapsulation of the ways readers have sought to explain what is challenging and paradoxical about Stein's writing, I am inclined to believe that Stein is not chiefly engaged in obfuscation. That readers often conclude so, however, is a telling phenomenon. Further, I would contend that the strategies identified by Gilbert and Gubar as "quite different"—sub/textual homosexuality and subversive deconstruction—in fact have a history of coexisting in such subcultural forms as camp and burlesque, where paradox stands at the center. Nonetheless, it is accurate to say that the history of Stein criticism has been dominated by efforts to explain rather than embrace experiences the reader finds unexpected or polyvalent about Stein's work. This chapter considers the reasons for and alternatives to that reader response.

From the outset of her career, Stein carried, perhaps deservedly so, a reputation as a "difficult" writer, one whose work did not respond readily to the genteel customs of reading. In her retrospective on Stein criticism, Marianne DeKoven correlates the formation of Stein's reputation for "unintelligibility" to the coincident rise of New Criticism, a mode of analysis that spurred critics such as Edmund Wilson, wielding New Criticism's criteria for literary taste, to judge Stein "queer and very boring" for the unconventional properties of her writing; in short, he ruled her differences errant.[5] While few readers encountering Stein's work for the first time, whether now or during her lifetime, would argue that Stein's writing is "easy," readers differ substantively in the way they perceive and respond to the challenges of her texts. Consider an example. Thornton Wilder, longtime friend and fellow writer, speaks to Stein's reputation for indeterminacy in his introduction to Stein's *Four in America*. He attributes at least some of the difficulty not to inattention to her audience but rather to prescience. He sees Stein's difference more benignly, as the result of immersion in a project many of her readers had not yet even thought to begin:

She knew that she was a difficult and an idiosyncratic author. She pursued her aims, however, with such conviction and intensity that occasionally she forgot that the results could be difficult to others. At such times the achievements she had made in writing, in "telling what she knew" (her most frequent formulation of the aim of writing) had to her the character of self-evident beauty and clarity. A friend, to whom she showed recently completed examples of her poetry, was frequently driven to reply sadly: "But you forget that I don't understand examples of your extremer styles." To this she would reply with a mixture of bewilderment, distress, and exasperation: "But what's the difficulty? Just read the words on the paper. They're in English. Just read them. Be simple and you'll understand these things."[6]

Wilder forgives Stein her singularity, then, and seeks to recuperate her work by demystifying it. Using Stein's frequent (and to some listeners' ears, disingenuous) retort to questioners, that the work requires only the reader's simple attention, Wilder contests the notion of Stein as extreme or inaccessible. She is available, he contends, to anyone willing to face the greatest challenge of all, given the expectations audience members accord an experimentalist—to "read the words on the paper."

If subsequent criticism offers an accurate indication, few readers chose to apply, or succeeded in applying, Wilder's advice to the engagement of Stein's texts. Even those who chose to write about her work tended to emphasize its properties of estrangement rather than familiarity, placing the exotic before the everyday, seeing her work as strange rather than simple. It would be quite some time until readers would begin to interrogate their own scripts of reading as a means better to engage Stein's work and their responses to it. Judy Grahn, a poet profoundly influenced by Stein's oeuvre, represents a case in point. Grahn's initial devotion to Stein did little to deepen her understanding until she interrogated her own expectations (her pre-texts, if you will) in approaching a Stein composition.

> For years I thought: "She is difficult," until one day it occurred to me to say it the other way: "She is easy. I am difficult."
>
> Suppose it is not that she is veiled and obscure but that we, her readers, are. We are veiled by our judgments. We come to writing prepared to compare it to other writing we have known. Since there is no one to compare her with, this method doesn't work for Gertrude Stein.
>
> We have been taught by most of our writers to expect certain functions of writing: that it models emotion for us, as blues singing also does, allowing us to explore feeling; that it provide tension-relief in the

form of solved mysteries, cliff-hanging adventures and will-she-won't-she romances; that it recreate foreign and exotic places, and fantasy landscapes; that we be reflected back to ourselves in sociological form or slice-of-life photographs. Stein's work does not perform any of these social functions nor did she ever intend that it would.

Stein spent much effort distinguishing for herself the difference between identity and essence. "Am I I because my little dog knows me?" she asked.

Or stated this way: Can I enter her or anyone's writing only if I already recognize myself and my own past experiences in it? Can I experience the writing as current event rather than reflection?

By suspending judgment about how a story, poem or play "should go" and by agreeing with myself to keep reading even when I can't find a way to recognize myself, I have begun to muddle into the landscape of her mind.[7]

As she chronicles her difficulties with reading Stein, Grahn enumerates some key preconceptions readers bring to literary texts—that they ought to afford readers the opportunity to emote, let go of tension, journey to fantasy locales, and see themselves mirrored. Along the way, Grahn also suggests that pervading our strategies for reading experimental texts, whether fittingly or not, are the formulas of representation and response associated with popular narrative forms such as the blues, mysteries, adventure fiction, and romances. Lodged as we are in a postmodern haze of appropriated images and forms, we have come to read everything, including "serious" literary texts, through the conventions we have internalized through (over)exposure to mass culture. Still, with Stein's work, that impulse might prove uniquely helpful.

Like Thornton Wilder's attempt to persuade us of Stein's simplicity, Grahn's discovery about the initial hardship experienced in reading Stein has more to do with the properties of the reader than the text: "She is easy. I am difficult." Grahn also articulates the peril and the promise of reading Stein differently: that without our customs as readers, we no longer know exactly who we are in the literary texts we inhabit. More threatening than the notion that we might not recognize her texts is the idea that, if we read Stein anew, we might no longer recognize ourselves as readers. We might not be immediately affirmed by illusions of literary mastery and meaning. We might, in short, take risks.

Still, in the fictional world Stein (de)constructs—for the most part, a world without characters in the realist sense, without heroes of any order, without the niceties of plot, rising action, dialogue, resolution, or closure—readers cannot be sure where they stand. Denied the usual ways of entering and traversing fiction (such as identification with a character or narrator), readers must somehow make something of Stein's texts. In this process, if readers do not forfeit the textual encounter altogether, they open up a collaboration with the writer and/or text. They help to write the text, to utter its stories, to construct (and dismantle), to reformulate its meanings. To engage with a Stein text, one must reconstitute oneself as a reading subject. Stein effects a reader's "conversion" paradoxically—by displacing the reader's faith in writers as authorities, narratives as absolute doctrines, and interpretations as rituals of tribute and affirmation. Stein insists on a resourceful, active reader, one willing to take part in the text's formation, to contribute rather than comply. It is not enough to perform an "audit" on the text, carefully assessing what is present and reckoning an account. Instead, one may activate her texts, which offer (partial, negotiable) scripts for response rather than (pristine, inviolate) artifacts for restatement.

Increasingly, critics such as Harriet Chessman have come to perceive this aspect of Stein's reconfigured contract between writer and reader in favorable terms, as an intimate dialogue:

> I interpret this challenge as urging us toward an open-ended and speculative responsiveness to her writing, resisting traditional critical claims to objectivity and closure, and allowing ample room for subjectivity. Stein encourages her "public" to form a certain intimacy with each composition and to engage in reading as a process filled with starts and stops, moments of confusion or uncertainty, and pleasure in the configurations of sound and possible significance as they appear to one's senses and imagination. Stein makes it difficult to master her writing or to enter into a relationship with the writing that could even figure mastery as a possibility.[8]

Important here are the central effects of readerly collaboration and textual reciprocity—that the writer no longer monopolizes meaning and the reader, in turn, no longer demands a single, unitary and fixed meaning of the text. Both parties in the contract must relinquish something for the sake of greater gains. If the reader truly collaborates, the writer no longer wields over an audience the final word on a text's implication. Neither does the author stand obliged to discipline the text such that it flatters the reader with the sensation of mastery in textual explication. In place of an orderly text, satisfyingly collected, is the prospect of a more ongoing relationship in which reader and writer perform their identities and test out their understandings of the text and one another, a testing complete with missteps, misunderstandings, gaps, pleasures, and sensual play.

Nancy Gray describes this re-visioned literary experience in ways similar to those used by Chessman: "We seem to be in it together, these words and I. Stein has chosen and has placed her words so that they make movement, a live presence. They slide and stop, turn and talk, invite me in and let me choose my own part in the composition while they are what they are, always there but never quite the same twice."[9] Gray's depiction underscores the sense in which the collaboration of reader and writer may stop but does not end. The text remains in movement rather than arriving at stasis. The reader's work does not conclude, because it does not move toward a fixed destination. Much like a spider's travel on a web, the resulting journey undertaken by the reader is anything but linear. Using language analogous to Ellen Berry's term, "textual wandering," Gray describes the reader's experience by imbuing Stein's words with animation; they "slide and stop, turn and talk."

In this regard, it seems no coincidence that the ways in which critics portray their engagement with Stein's texts are kinesthetic and theatrical in diction: a "dance," a "living presence," a "current event rather than reflection." There is a sense in which all of Stein's texts, whether marked as plays or not, are most alive (and we to them) as performances. The more one reads her, the more one sounds the language, visualizes movements, and partakes of the dramatic play implied by the concept of dialogue. As Jane Palatini Bowers puts it, "Whether the work is a narrative, a lyric or a drama, it is ultimately a performance by Gertrude Stein, the writer. Stein invents a kind of 'process poetics' that informs all of her work."[10] If Stein delivers a surprising performance as the "author," we must also enact our identities as readers in ways we did not anticipate. Across the pages, we play out scenes—literary, critical, theoretical.

With time, we make it less our object to affix an identity to Stein or a scripted implication to her work, and more our object to imagine how to unfix identities and improvise our findings. This performative mode in reading Stein has been advocated by Lisa Ruddick in her review essay, "Stein and Cultural Criticism in the Nineties," in which she speculates about the future of Stein scholarship, noting that "a hopeful prediction is that the concept of 'performativity' which is coursing through cultural studies at the moment penetrates more deeply and multiply into Stein criticism in the next few years."[11] A performative approach to Stein makes it possible for us to read through uncertainty in ways that prove compelling, empowering, and yes, feminist.

A reader's uncertainties are no longer regarded as sites of failures but rather as liminal ground, where new possibilities take shape. As Henry Sayre has written of the role of uncertainty in the work of one Stein-influenced figure, mixed-media/performance artist Laurie Anderson,

> Not only do the media themselves collide but so do the work's possible meanings. "In all the work I've ever done," Anderson explains, "my whole intention was not to map out meanings but to make a field situation. I'm interested in facts, images and theories which resonate against each other, not in offering solutions." This notion of the performance as a sort of "field situation" emphatically ties the audience into the problematics of the event itself, involving them in the dilemmas she presents. Anderson perpetually creates scenarios which baffle us or show us how the landscape of our daily lives—a landscape so banal that we tend to take it for granted—can suddenly transform itself into disorienting and mysterious terrain.[12]

Through the "field situation" of Stein's unruly texts, readers move into the frame not merely as consumers of ready-made fantasies but rather as producers of active responses, transgressive poses, and moments of transforming vision. If we can perform in an improvisational manner, prepared to encounter confusion creatively and build it into the collaboration, we may begin to read anew what Stein calls "the words on the paper." We may not always recognize ourselves in these performances, as Grahn has warned, but we may nonetheless thrive on what we see and become along the way.

As I introduce my own readings of Stein's work, a few words about how I see may be in order. My analytical method bears the influence of a variety of theoretical frameworks, including reader-response, feminist, contextual, and deconstructive criticisms. My previous Stein scholarship has involved close readings of texts considered to be among her most difficult pieces, such as *The Making of Americans*, "Lend a Hand or Four Religions," *Lucy Church Amiably*, and *Four Saints in Three Acts*. It is my hope that by viewing Stein's texts and readers in the context of one another and in light of recent movements in cultural studies, revisionist approaches to the concept of modernism, theories of gender and reading, and issues in queer theory, an examination of Stein's forays into popular culture may bring depth, nuance, and a renewed sense of possibility to the process of reading Gertrude Stein.

The chief objectives for this volume, then, are: (1) to explore the interdependence of literary practice and literary theory within Stein's work, (2) to investigate the implications of Stein's fascination with mass culture/popular culture and its expressive modes, both for the composition and reception of her texts, (3) to bring forward culturally contextualized criticism of little-studied Stein texts, (4) to situate Stein's work in relation to (and in contest with) familiar literary genres, particularly short fiction, (5) to reckon the role literary camp plays within Stein's writing, and (6) to make available and relevant key companion and critical texts informing examination of Stein's short fiction.

The portion of this book devoted to my analysis of Stein's short fiction appears in the form of eight chapters. The first three chapters open up the process of reading her work as reader-activated, available for collaborative acts of meaning. This introduction concentrates on what it means to read Stein today. The second chapter is a discussion of what it might mean to read Stein's work mindful of its relationship to literary genres, such as short fiction. Using the example of Stein's *The Making of Americans,* the discussion explores Stein's reputation as a genre-buster.[13] The third chapter examines Stein's relationship to a wide range of popular forms, literary and otherwise, setting out some thoughts about the implication of Stein's travels across the high-pop-cultural divide usually associated with modernism. The fourth, fifth, and sixth chapters (each titled with Stein's signature gerunds, forms of "being") offer case studies, each addressing a specific popular literary form in its relation to Stein's writing practices and its implication for readers of Stein: detective stories, children's tales, and love stories. The fourth chapter looks at Stein's concern with the detective genre, especially as expressed through her novella, *Blood on the Dining-Room Floor.*[14] In the fifth chapter, I construct a reading of Stein's take on children's fiction, *The World Is Round.*[15] Following that essay is a third case study, in which I consider Stein's erotic writings, particularly "Didn't Nelly and Lilly Love You," in terms of the romance as genre.[16] The remaining chapters place these close readings in the context of the history of reception of Stein's texts. The seventh chapter builds from the preceding essays and case studies to identify possibilities for locating her short fiction in the context of literary camp. Finally, "What Becomes a Legend: Reading the Popular in Gertrude Stein," furnished as a conclusion to this study of Stein's short fiction, focuses on the ways in which and ends toward which readers—particularly those outside the academy—have received and appropriated both Stein's prose and persona.

Part 1

After spending a number of years reading, discussing, teaching, and writing about the work of Gertrude Stein, I find it a pleasure to prepare a book of introduction to her writing. I have found that Stein's work is not as widely known as one might suppose given the familiarity of her name and image in the popular culture. Even many avid readers can summon no more than the oft-quoted line, "A rose is a rose is a rose." The bulk of her work, the legacy of a prolific writer, goes unremarked and, in large measure, unread. In the past 25 years, however, there has been a resurgence in interest in Stein among literary critics. She has, in particular, been invoked by Language poets, feminist critics, and those who regard her as a precursor to postmodernism in writing. Nonetheless, there remains a tremendous opportunity to discover, explore, enjoy, and construct innovative readings using Stein's texts. If you have never read Stein, have read one or two of her more accessible texts (such as *Three Lives* or *The Autobiography of Alice B. Toklas*), or have learned considerably more through wide reading of Stein, you have the chance to contribute to our understanding of Stein's work—provided that you are prepared to delight in it. For while many insist that her writing is difficult, even impenetrable, I tend to endorse Stein's own instruction for engaging her texts: "If you enjoy it you understand it."[17] If we attempt to read her work through our customary strategies, we may indeed be foiled. If we dare to improvise and read the texts on their own (very different and dialogical) terms, we may instead find pleasure and insight. Let it be so. What follows are my efforts to read Gertrude Stein's texts experimentally or, in the sense-grounded words of Stein, a record of how "Watts looked in listening."[18] May the conversation continue.

Genre and Gertrude Stein

> But first what is poetry and what is prose. I wonder if I can
> tell you.
> —Gertrude Stein, "Poetry and Grammar"

As previously stated, Stein's work intervenes in the traditionally implied literary contract between writer and reader, and this intervention can be a feature rather than a flaw of our readings of Stein. She challenges readers to reimagine such paradigms of literary study as form and genre through alternative reading and writing practices. Perhaps it is because of Stein's complicated relationship to genre categories—writing on/across the boundaries of poetry, drama, autobiography, fiction, philosophical treatise, art manifesto, fairy tale, love story, memoir, essay, lecture, and opera—that relatively few existing studies of Stein's work have ventured to speak of it in relation to familiar literary genres. Instead, the tendency has been to offer general commentaries on the work, readings of individual texts, or examinations of groupings of texts that appear together to reflect a nonliterary genre (her portraits, for example). To the best of my knowledge, no published work has attended to Stein's relationship to the genre of short fiction. It is precisely because of Stein's function as a genre-buster, though, that it becomes useful to reflect on the ways in which Stein simultaneously invokes and subverts the notion of literary genre and enlivens that notion through contact with the narrative strategies and forms commonly associated with mass media and popular culture.

In particular, then, this book focuses on Stein's relationship to the genre of short fiction, a relationship that seems always to have been a vexed question. Even among Stein scholars there is no consensus about the assignment of her writings to genres such as plays, poems, and works of fiction. That is, while most agree that she worked in each of these forms, debates arise when it comes to individual pieces and their identification with particular genres. Surely Stein fuels these disputes through her distinctive and parodic writing practices. It was not unusual for her to subtitle a piece only one page in length "A Novel." Book-

13

length works of fiction, such as Stein's *Three Lives,* may as easily be considered as collections of short stories. Her short compositions may have endless chapter divisions, while her longer pieces may proceed without interruption. Stein plays fast and loose with the protocols associated with genre forms, and this play begins to function as a metanarrative, a commentary about literary genres and literary theory conducted right in the literary texts. In her criticism Stein pronounces the novel dead, but she continues to write novels. She names the poetic tradition as patriarchal and goes on to inscribe her matronym nonetheless. She claims that only passé writers receive recognition in their prime, and yet she declares herself the great literary mind of the twentieth century. She writes and publishes someone *else's* autobiography. After that, she presumes to compose what she calls *Everybody's Autobiography.*[19] What's an audience to do? If readers have found her writings hard to love, they are harder still to classify.

The ways in which Stein's work defies genre classification become even more apparent in today's age of computer-assisted library retrieval. Within a single CD-ROM index, the *MLA Bibliography,* Stein's book-length *Ida* appears alternately categorized as novel, poetry, drama, and short story. It is difficult to assign single and unitary generic names to Stein's texts, a difficulty that might well be a component of the reader's challenge issued by Stein. The difficulty in ordering Stein's texts in generic terms at once suggests the irrelevance and the intransigence of such schemes of categorization. Critics attest to this challenge to the reader, as when one notes how, "Again and again, Stein will do this in her novels, novelle, and short stories, give us just enough of the conventions associated with the genre to convince us of what we are reading before she begins to stretch one's capacity for seeing, hearing, and believing."[20]

There is first the question of Stein's titling of works (often via mock-genre designations), then the matter of how critics engaging the works regard literary genre. Furthermore, a reader's reliance on genre classifications may cause her or him to bypass more active strategies for textual engagement. That is, custom dictates that with every literary genre go reader's recipes for constituting meaning with the text. ("When reading a murder mystery, the reader undertakes to uncover the identity of the person/s responsible for the murder at the center of the story.") These habits of reading and perception threaten to reinforce rather than contest readers' previous notions and expectations about literary structure and meaning, as well as their preconceived ideas about the way persons, relationships, and events are or should be. Stein, however, called upon her readers to see, and then see beyond, category or form. For Stein, the twentieth century could no longer afford simple reliance on such formulas of meaning.

For instance, Stein was reluctant to use the term *story* to describe anything she wrote. Perhaps the word conjured a form too representational, too causal in its structures, too character-driven, too linear in its telling, too closed in its plot, too wedded to a beginning, middle, and ending, and so too limited in its possibilities for her tastes. She was careful to remind readers that the only important fiction of her time—and there were only three titles on her list (*Remembrance of Things Past, Ulysses,* and *The Making of Americans*)—did not, in her view, burden themselves or their readers with story.

In place of the term *story* or *fiction,* Stein was fond of calling her writings, particularly those composed after *The Autobiography of Alice B. Toklas,* narratives. This term proved more to her liking. It seemed better to describe the modern audience's needs, for Stein believed that readers no longer cared for or about literary characters in the ways they had during the nineteenth century. She believed that publicity, with its celebrities, had eroded the passion for literary characters in the public's imagination, and so literature could no longer take its energy from the reader's connection to characters. If writers did not reckon with this reality of the mass media age, they would be doomed to failure. As a result of the shift to a consumer culture defined by advertising and publicity, "the novel," she argued, "is not a living form, and people try to get out of the difficulty by essay and short story form, and that is a feeble form at best."[21]

Of course, these dire pronouncements about the state of novel, essay, and short story in no way prevented Stein from appropriating and reinventing these literary forms. Indeed, the challenge of animating these genres seemed to intrigue her. In her efforts to meet that challenge, Stein turned to the very forms of modernity she argued had destroyed nineteenth-century fiction, the narrative modes of popular and mass culture. Despite her reputation as a difficult and even esoteric experimentalist, Stein demonstrated an abiding interest in narrative forms and strategies at work in mass culture, and this fascination found its way into many of her own writings. This book analyzes issues surrounding Stein's preoccupation with popular and mass-cultural expressive forms (including advertising, heroic biography, romance, detective and mystery fiction, etiquette literature, film, photography, radio, novellas and novelettes, primers, and newspapers), as well as the implication of these interests for her own writings both within and across existing literary genres.

Indeed, in positioning her own work, Stein seems deeply interested in the distinctions to be made between the nineteenth and twentieth centuries. Unconvinced that the shift from one century to the other actually occurred in 1900, Stein offers her own counterhypothesis. She was fond of saying that the Civil War, not the millennium, had ushered in the twentieth century. At her most narcissistic, she claims that she herself (more exactly, her opus, *The Making of Americans*) had brought about the new century. This Stein text represents in microcosm the ways in which the writer contests the nineteenth century's hold on fiction, displacing the literary conventions of realism to bring about a more modern form of narrative for the twentieth century. In this early Stein composition, one finds a casebook for resisting and redirecting a literary inheritance in all its particulars: genre, plot, dramatic structure, perspective, characterization, and more.

The Making of Americans is the volume Gertrude Stein claimed had begun modern writing. While it is clearly in some measure a work of fiction, Stein's *The Making of Americans* resists conventional literary classification. While some critics regard it as a novel, it may be better characterized as a daybook, containing literary sketches, reflections, and frequently, as is the case in many of her later compositions, a running commentary on the text's own writing. No short story, this piece, some 550,000 words and 925 pages in its unabridged form, represents nearly eight years of work by Stein (1902–1911). Portions of the text, about 150 pages written early in the process, appeared in serial fashion in the *Transatlantic*, a periodical of the day. Both the text's bulk and its literary irregularities made Stein's efforts to publish *The Making of Americans* in book form an arduous task, finally accomplished in 1925. An abridged version, with trimming done by Stein herself, appeared in 1934. It would be many years before the full text of this work would become available in print once more.

Many readers have observed that at the same time Stein's *The Making of Americans* appears to pose as a novel, the text also devotes itself to defying many conventional expectations readers bring to novels. It has been cast alternately as the Great American Novel and as that genre's most audacious parody. It is for this reason that criticism of the text tends to dwell on Stein's dispensing with the customs of novel writing. The text departs from tradition in several important regards. It does not conform to a reader's anticipation of a focus on events or happenings that generally form a novel's plot. Stein built an ambivalent and unorthodox relationship to plot. In her lectures and writings about literature, Stein would contend that events do not make literature, so why pretend that they sustain fiction's forward movement? While it can generally be said that something happens in Stein's writings, there is no gesture toward conventional dramatic schemes of rising, climaxing, and falling action.

Where the text does describe action, its movements seldom appear in the order they occurred, according to the sequence of linear time. Stein actively moved away from the literary formula of a text's beginning, middle, and end. Furthermore, events at issue in her texts do not unfold as one might expect; when events appear in Stein's work, they fold, unfold, and fold again. Along with her aversion to elaborately stated plots, Stein saw little reason to emphasize events. Reportage was, at best, the work of other media, such as newspapers. Literary writing, by contrast, should not take its direction from events. In the most important works of fiction, Stein maintained, nothing happens. Their dramas and disclosures travel not from events but rather from crises of identity and relationship, matters without tidy causal explanations.

Stein's literary characters remain similarly elusive; they rarely receive development as might be thought typical of fiction, sometimes remain unnamed, and at other times share the names of other figures already established in the text. Patterning of the text around the characters whose names the text's component books bear is often as a nominal subject rather than as an explanatory gesture toward the section's subject matter. Even the work's final book, echoing with its name the novel's subtitle, "Being a History of a Family's Progress," declines to function as a means of establishing textual closure, and so there is no explicit restoration of order among the story's events, resolution of its conflicts, or testament to progress. In literary characters, Stein claimed there could no longer be any real reader interest. Celebrities had taken the place of fictional figures in the imaginative lives of the public. As a result, in the bulk of Stein's fiction, characters may be identified through pronouns or nicknames. Comparatively few appear identified by their given names. Interpersonal relationships are explored in rather more detail, but the individual identities remain blurry. It is possible to argue that the most dimensional characters in Stein's fiction remain the writer and the reader, twin protagonists in a metafiction of their transactions through the text.

Along with its other refusals of storytelling techniques, Stein's text also complicates novelistic devices for establishing narrative perspective. *The Making of Americans* does not, for instance, rely on one continuous speaking voice. It does not frame its contents with a single, governing point of view. It does not permit the reader to enter an uncritical relationship to the teller/s of the tale. Questions of the narrative's pose, perspective, and credibility never come to rest in the text. The reader is left to moderate the text's voices in order to receive the stories it claims to tell.

In addition to resisting these literary conventions, this Stein text also challenges cultural conventions, particularly concerning social difference and its representation. For instance, *The Making of Americans* explores typologies of human character. This characterological interest may have carried over from Stein's early interest in psychology, forged through college study and laboratory research. What accounts for the gap between person and personae? What types of people could be said to populate the United States? Is there such a thing as a national character? How do people's personalities shape their interactions and relationships? How do the structures of the traditional family help create character? How do people encounter difference? These are the issues underlying Stein's text, charging her writing with an energy that comes not from the fulfillment of the novel's generic form but rather from efforts to dislodge harmful literary and cultural assumptions.

Although *The Making of Americans* corresponds closely (on many points) to events in Stein's and her family's history, this novel does more than chronicle the author's family history, for it also tells the more general story of "old people in a new world." Issues of race, class, ethnicity, gender, and religion all play a part. Stein not only represents the experience of the transplanted business-class family, as suggested by her own origin, but also depicts the lives of the working class and service professions. Therefore, while the lived perspective of the author is that of one accustomed to privilege, Stein makes an effort to include (albeit through elite eyes) the lives of seamstresses, governesses, servants, and their families. As a result, *The Making of Americans* is rich with the social relations of class. Indeed, critic Clive Bush has called *The Making of Americans* "a 'romantic satire'—on the psychopathology of an emerging mass society." He goes on to locate the text as a critique of bourgeois complacency:

> Stein's shrewd gaze focuses on the apparent success of the bourgeois revolution in America: on the American Dream, no less, with its

utopian goal of freedom based on property ownership, its sharp demar-
cation of male-female roles, its triumph of the average, its psychology
of the middle way, its individualism, and its claim to have solved the
dynamic of nature and labour through honest business practice, cul-
tured leisure and moderated passion within family life.[22]

Tendering a critique of the bourgeois habits economist Thorstein
Veblen termed "conspicuous consumption," and its attendant practices
of materialism, commodification of others, and maintenance of the status quo, Stein's *The Making of Americans* is not just an attempt to modernize literature by directing attention to mass culture and its forms but
also a commentary on the foibles and conservatism of a modernity
defined through acquisition and social position.[23] In particular, the text
appears to problematize the matters of identity in a society so constituted. Identity—whether one's own or that of others—becomes a very
open and troubling question.

In this regard, Stein's *Making of Americans* provides a study of human
perception, concentrating on the ways in which members of different
segments of society view each other. Stein makes this point comedically
in a passage purporting to state her authorial intentions: "First there
will be the impression everyone had of them then and the history of
their living and then there will be a reconstruction of the four of them
from the memory of the impression of them and then a reconstruction
of the father and the mother out of the reconstructed four children"
(*TMOA*, 261). Stein's terminology within this passage, especially her
choice of terms such as "impression," "memory," and "reconstruction,"
suggests she is more concerned with subjective experience of historical
reality than with construction of a unitary narrative more characteristic
of the generational saga. She transforms that literary form from a heroic
testament to progress and filial pride into a rather scathing satire of ideological scripts and comforting cultural fictions such as America as melt-
ing pot, rags-to-riches tales from Horatio Alger, and national claims to
liberty and justice for all.

Stein's own family history could be mapped as a traditional story of
immigrants finding material success in America. Furthermore, although
she was born in the United States, Stein might have felt herself something of an immigrant. She spent much of her childhood moving around,
and many of her formative years were spent in Europe. At the very least,
she lived among immigrants and so was familiar with the expectations of
opportunity and achievement they brought with them to the new land.

In some ways, it seems only natural that Martha Hersland, the character most closely corresponding to Gertrude Stein in this somewhat autobiographical fiction, should see issues of cultural difference, such as ethnicity, in terms of her family's servants. Like her affluent character, Stein probably got her first extended exposure to class and ethnic differences through servants in the Steins' employ (including her Czechoslovakian tutor and Hungarian governess). With the character of Martha Hersland, Stein points out that a child raised in a middle- or upper-class home often knows the household staff better than she or he knows her or his relations. The children may spend most of their time and receive most of their care from servants whose background is likely to be different from theirs. Stein's gestures toward depicting a cross section of society lead the author to sketch out (and, in her notebooks, literally diagram) men and women in an effort to render each character complete, regardless of their social standing.

These efforts seem to be informed by a democratic impulse. Stein describes herself as singular in terms of her interest in all walks of life, and within the text, she portrays the solitude in which she must work as a result. Because Stein anticipates the difficulty an elite audience will have accepting such characterizations, she concludes that, "I write for myself and strangers" (*TMOA*, 289). In this respect, Stein anticipates recent discussions of cultural "otherness," for if *The Making of Americans* is written *for* strangers, it is written also *about* strangers, a group in which she was quick to include herself ("queer things like us" [*TMOA*, 47]).

Within her effort to write what she calls "a history of every one," Stein begins to offer explanations for the human differences she observes. Given its focus on immigrant life, *The Making of Americans* has to do with issues of ethnicity as well as class, and as the novel's subtitle indicates, the process of cultural assimilation. *The Making of Americans* also shows Stein's sensitivity to the ways in which issues of class and ethnicity interlock. While Stein retains ethnicity and class as central categories in her analysis of human character, she demonstrates how inseparable from such an examination of ethnicity and class is the matter of religious belief. Stein warns that when an individual seeks to impose beliefs and prescribe actions, religion becomes the pretext for oppression, in which the faithful seek to control others. Stein also argues that to believe in anything too much is to see that belief become dogma.

As Stein begins to highlight power asymmetries within the family and the society, she also offers a critique of the gender roles implied by patriarchy. For example, women in *The Making of Americans* come to recognize that their husbands pose as masters toward the wives in much the way those same men regard servants—as if they owned them. As the text proceeds, Stein valorizes women with the capacity to engage critically with belief, to empower themselves by resisting dogma, and to wage a struggle against all forms of oppression.

Stein's disruption of writer's conventions and readers' expectations inspires a heightened awareness of language as a cultural practice. Her experimental writings affected numerous modernists of her day, and she maintained that high modernists Marcel Proust and James Joyce had copied *The Making of Americans.* Her work spanned virtually every literary form, and in the spirit of the modernist move toward irreverence, Stein engaged in many acts of genre-blurring, genre-blending, and genre-busting. These innovations call attention to habits of perception and expression, including those divisions associated with various forms of social difference, performance of identity, stigma, and inequality.

While critics have been thorough in cataloguing Stein's textual irregularities, they disagree about the implications of this unconventional writing. Many feminist critics contend that language represents and serves the existing social order, chiefly by supporting and contributing to oppression based upon differences such as gender, race, class, ethnicity, and religion. Writings for social change, therefore, may need to confront the conservative nature of language as an instrument. Decades before these contemporary feminist critics, Stein maintained that a writer's cultural critiques are usefully targeted at language itself. Within her unconventional writings, Stein reclaims existing language by creating oppositional strategies to the hierarchy and patriarchy encoded within that language.

Although Stein's readers have endeavored to place her work in the context of existing literary forms and genres, she claimed to give such considerations little attention. "It is the critics who have really thought about form always," Stein maintained, "and I have thought about—writing!"[24] It may not be possible or even necessary to locate each of Stein's compositions within the frameworks of literary classifications such as genre. Stein regarded such preoccupations as deadening to the writer and her work. In fact, when asked by interviewer John Preston what she noticed about American writers, Stein spoke of the ways in which self-consciousness about literary form constrained them. The result, she argued, is that by a certain age, "Something goes out of them and they begin to repeat according to formula. Or else they grow silent altogether" (Preston, 158). If a writer becomes too concerned to write within the boundaries of existing literary forms, the work loses its evocative power, its voice.

With her own writing, Stein stretched, stroked, pierced, and plucked at those generic boundaries, all the while writing that process of disruption into her texts as a kind of declaration of independence from literary precedent. The result is a textured metanarrative about the ways in which language should not be permitted to limit or contain expression, as with the boundaries of literary and social categories. There is seldom a sense that Stein's writing is propelled by a central action and its consequences. If one were to insist, however, on such a model of plot, then it would involve the process of the text's reading. The reader, as a metanarrative's protagonist, initiates the story's action and closes it. The reader constructs the story of the text's production. In these terms, as Shari Benstock writes, "Analysis of genres, names, pronomial categories, and verbal constructions provide a (Sapphic) plot to the Stein *oeuvre*."[25]

With this monumental novel, *The Making of Americans*, Stein claimed she had done something truly new. She characterized the nineteenth century as full of convictions—progress, evolution, religion, hope of a global language—the twentieth century would place in doubt. Indeed, Stein saw herself duty bound to challenge the nineteenth century's faith in such beliefs. In this version of literary history, which she often narrated as a story of generations, Stein characterized her obligation as nothing short of patricide. Her literary generation could not afford to let the previous one remain. It was her role to "kill" the nineteenth century and rid literature of its assumptions and complacencies.[26]

Of course, Stein did not need to kill what was already dead. As her comments about Proust and Joyce suggest, fiction required revival. Stein described short fiction as a weak form, the novel a dead one. Indeed, at times, she pronounced all such literary genres lifeless, explaining that "all those forms are dead because they have become forms" (Preston, 165). Only three writers, according to Stein, gave fiction life again and, in doing so, gave us the twentieth century: Joyce, Proust, and Stein. According to Stein, this modern life must begin with the death of the old—by shedding the literary and cultural residue of the past. The nineteenth century must die for the twentieth to live. In this measure, Stein took up the role of assassin early in her career, but it remained to be seen if Stein had committed the perfect murder. As she equivocated in the final sentence of *The Geographical History of America*, "I am not sure that is not the end."[27]

Stein, Narrative, and Mass Culture

> I like ordinary people who don't bore me. Highbrows, you
> know, always do.
> —Gertrude Stein, quoted by James Mellow,
> *Dictionary of Literary Biography*

This chapter locates Stein's interest in the media of American popular culture in relation to her own writing practices and modes. Stein struggled throughout her career with questions of audience and popularity. As a person, Stein relished privacy; as a writer, she detested anonymity. Although deeply suspicious of the potentially deleterious effect of fame on both her life and her writing, Gertrude Stein enjoyed a complicated relationship to the literary marketplace and, with it, consumer culture—characterized largely by a commingling of ardor, envy, and dread. She wanted her works read, not merely collected or remarked. She wanted her writing to be prized not just by the *literati* but also by a wider readership. By her own admission, part of the thrill she felt in reading popular literary forms—mysteries, romances, novelettes, and the like—was in the realization that these works found so many readers in the general population. At the same time that she delighted in the words on their pages, she also wrote as someone profoundly jealous of such writers' ability to command and sustain a large popular audience.

As the following three chapters demonstrate, Gertrude Stein's writing responds to and reworks popular culture on many levels—thematic, intertextual, subcultural, and narrative. She was not afraid to seem low-brow in these enthusiasms. In this respect and others, she did not seem overly concerned about appearing out of step with other writers or even with other modernists. She welcomed the pleasures of texts, popular and otherwise, and did not rank the sources of these joys. She seemed only to hope that, as a writer, she might herself know the gratification of popularity. For the first decades of her career, that hope seemed improbable. Most of her work remained unpublished and unknown.

Thanks to the popular success of *The Autobiography of Alice B. Toklas* and the theatrical production of *Four Saints in Three Acts*, however, all that would change.[28] The 1930s marked a sharp upturn in Stein's visibility. During the last two decades of her life and career, Stein got to experience her own form of celebrity. It was in these days that her embrace of mass-cultural forms was first returned. After the best-selling *Autobiography,* its serialization in the *Atlantic Monthly,* and its identification as a Literary Guild selection, Stein was happy to report that her name appeared in *Who's Who.* While still in Paris, Stein received tokens of the advent of her long-awaited fame. One such tribute came via a 1934 letter from Carl Van Vechten, photo enclosed, showing a Gimbel's department store display inspired by the performance of Stein's operatic collaboration with Virgil Thomson, *Four Saints in Three Acts.* The photograph depicted a shopwindow of women's wear, boasting "4 Suits in 2 Acts." Gimbel's also sold tablecloths inspired by "Four Saints." Stein was overjoyed. She had relished bookstore displays of her works, as when she reports, for instance, in the *Autobiography,* her pleasure in seeing a *Lucy Church Amiably* window arrangement in Paris. Still, there had never been so close before her—as the department-store spoofs seemed to suggest—the prospect of achieving a household name.

It would not be the last such experience for Stein. Following the publication of the *Autobiography* and initial performances of *Four Saints,* Stein agreed to conduct a lecture tour in the United States. This transatlantic journey, undertaken after a 31-year absence from the nation of her birth, brought Stein and Toklas to the States on 24 October 1934. They were greeted with considerable fanfare. On her arrival in New York, she and Toklas were announced with a message on the scrolling lightboard in Times Square. Before that day was out, she would be filmed for a Pathé newsreel. As their stay proceeded, she would be interviewed on the radio and recorded on archival voice recordings as she read her work aloud. She would be photographed by such notables as Carl Van Vechten. She would stand before large groups assembled across the United States to hear her comment on her own work. Before she returned to Paris, these talks would be published as *Lectures in America.* She would meet with students and university classes. She would attend live performances of her theatrical pieces, including *Four Saints in Three Acts* and *Capital Capitals.* She would contract with the *Herald Tribune* for a series of articles on "The American Scene." She would make headlines and attend countless teas, meals, parties, and book signings. On the basis of her name and request, she could make the acquaintance of her favorite cinema stars, request tea with First Lady Eleanor Roosevelt, or travel Chicago in a ride-along with the homicide squad. There now seemed every indication that, although it had taken some time for Stein to find such acclaim, she had finally arrived. Even if her fame was matched with notoriety (as the "Mama of Dada," the "Sibyl of Montparnasse," the "High Priestess," "The Enigma in the Woodpile," and "Grand Duchess of Literary 'What's It All About-dom' "), she could no longer feel overlooked—at worst, just misunderstood and underestimated. Her name, although perhaps not yet her work, emerged from literary obscurity.

After touring the States, Stein found it possible to publish more of her work. In conversations with a famous publisher, Stein maintained that her warm reception on that tour owed at least as much to her non-linear texts as it did to works such as *The Autobiography of Alice B. Toklas.* "Harcourt was very surprised when I said to him on first meeting him in New York remember this extraordinary welcome that I am having does not come from the books of mine that they do understand like the Auto-biography but the books of mine that they did not understand and he called his partner and said listen to what she says and perhaps after all she is right" (*EA,* 8). This process, though, due in large part to the effects of delayed recognition and compensation on a prolific writer, took decades. It was not until the 1950s, well after Stein's death from cancer in 1946, that many of her writings found their way into print through a Yale Press series. Following these eight book-length releases, interest in Stein's work quieted for a while. It was not until the 1970s that feminist readers started to retrieve her texts and her role in women's literary history. To this day, however, some Stein texts are known only to those who have ventured to special collections of her writing at research facilities such as Yale University's Beinecke Library.

Many more readers have turned to such books as *Narration, How Writing Is Written,* and *How to Write* for insights into Stein's notions of literary practice and theory.[29] The titles of these works suggest that they will elucidate such matters, and so readers expect to find there explanations for features found in her work. Frustrating such efforts is the fact that Stein's works always combine a concept with its example, a theory with its demonstration—and these three books are no exception. Whatever their titles seem to promise, these works call upon the reader to labor and reflect in much the same way her other texts require. They explore rather than explain, they complicate rather than enumerate, the underlying principles at work in Stein's writing. They reward only rigor in the reader. If one is to engage creatively the question of genre in Gertrude Stein, it is necessary to consider her work through her gestures in offering it to readers.

Of these works, the volume of Stein's writings published as *Narration* likely represents her most extended discussion of the interplay of popular culture and the literary marketplace. Here and in *Everybody's Autobiography,* Stein goes on record about storytelling as it operates in a wide range of contemporary expressive forms—journalism, dime novels, cinema, popular ballads, pulp fiction, advertising and publicity, and radio dramas. The writer's own work speaks to these cultural interests and influences. Stein claimed that her writing was shaped by street and automobile sounds. She toyed with slogans on billboards and advertisements, finding herself both fascinated and repelled by the narrative forms associated with print advertisement. Although she took inspiration from mass culture, in her work she ultimately tried to "tell" something that newspapers, advertisements, and radio programs could not, and in a way they could or would not.

Stein's work, with its movement away from linear plot, increasingly offered moments of recognition rather than satisfying progressions toward narrative closure. In this regard, her writing bears a resemblance to the medium of photography with its single frames. In much the same way that Henri Cartier-Bresson spoke and wrote of the decisive moment in photography, Stein creates glimpses—of irony, disjuncture, and surprise—rather than contexts, causalities, and explanations. Like Cartier-Bresson's photographs, Stein's word-pictures are images out of, rather than in, time. Stein's "continuous present" in writing parallels the eternal "now" of still photography. F. Richard Thomas has written in some detail about Stein as a literary admirer of Alfred Stieglitz.[30] Indeed, Stieglitz had published Stein's portraits early on in *Camera Work.*

In addition to her affinity for photography, Stein was also intrigued by the kindred medium of cinema. She writes of popular forms, and in particular the film genre, with no small bit of envy how "It was romantic . . . that the cheapest thing is made with the most care and the highest-paid creators are those that make that thing. It is romantic. Perhaps Hollywood too is that thing" (*EA,* 232). It may be that some of Stein's interest in Hollywood stemmed from her own desire for celebrity. After all, when Max Ewing wrote to Stein following the publication of *The Autobiography of Alice B. Toklas,* he assured the writer "you are more discussed in Hollywood these days than Greta Garbo."[31] Stars in Beverly Hills wanted to know Stein's publicity secret.

Allusions within her writing and events in her life suggest that Stein had more than a casual interest in Hollywood. She sought out opportunities to meet screen writers and stars such as Anita Loos, Mary Pickford, Charlie Chaplin, Dashiell Hammett, and Lillian Hellman. She praised Leon Wilson's cinema-inspired yet disenchanted novel, *Merton of the Movies,* as America's best tale of a young man. She longed to see her writings adapted to the screen, claimed to have been approached by Lillian May Ehrman about making a film of "The Gentle Lena" (from *Three Lives*), and lobbied powerful friends to arrange a film of *The Autobiography of Alice B. Toklas.* In her correspondence with Samuel Steward, Stein mentions, evidently with some pride, an agent's inquiry about adapting *The World is Round* to film.[32] She also acknowledged that film had influenced her writing forms, owning that she had written two movies, both published in *Operas and Plays.*[33] Critic Beth Hutchison has written of Stein's film scenarios, *A Movie* and *Film: Deux soeurs qui ne sont pas soeurs,* exploring the interstices of filmic and literary modes within these works.[34]

One telling incident in Stein's encounter with the film medium bears close examination, as it encapsulates the complicated relationship Stein enjoyed with mass culture. While in the States for her lecture tour, Stein delivered talks including "What is English Literature," "Pictures," "Plays," "The Gradual Making of *The Making of Americans,*" "Portraits and Repetition," and "Poetry and Grammar." Between these speaking engagements, Stein indulged her curiosities about 1930s America and what it had to offer culturally. While planning her California tour dates, Stein was asked whom she might care to meet at an upcoming dinner party. Among those Stein identified by name was Charlie Chaplin, the beloved tramp of silent film fame. Stein had seen Chaplin on the screen and evidently wished in particular to make his acquaintance while in California.

Thanks to an obliging hostess, the meeting took place. As it happens, both Stein and Chaplin recorded the occasion of their meeting in autobiographical writings. The two seem to remember the exchange rather differently, though. As the story most often is retold, and as it is recounted in Alice B. Toklas's *What Is Remembered,* Toklas greeted Chaplin by saying that she and Stein had seen only films by Chaplin. The account provided by biographer Janet Hobhouse, in *Everybody Who Was Anybody,* heightens this flattery, indicating that Stein and Toklas, having seen one Chaplin film, vowed never to return to the cinema, as nothing could rival Chaplin's work (Hobhouse, 191). At any rate, by the time that Toklas wrote her memoir, she ventured to disclose in retrospect that her compliment as spoken to Chaplin "was not exactly exact."[35]

Where the Stein and Chaplin accounts really diverge, however, is on the substance of their discussions that evening. Stein recalls the meeting fondly, as a talk between kindred souls. Her narrative focuses on their conversation about the ways in which silent film, freed as the medium was of the human voice, was capable of supporting a narrative form untethered by the tempo of spoken language (*EA*, 283). In other words, silent film had fluid rhythms and could move as quickly as the beholding eye could register its movement; silent pictures, then, did not have to reproduce actual duration. With the advent of sound, however, film's sights and sounds became synchronized and so could no longer break from the temporal rhythms of the lived world. Stein seemed to conclude that Chaplin shared her disappointment in this lost potential of the silent medium. In sum, Stein represents the conversation as cordial and thoughtful.

In his *Autobiography,* Charlie Chaplin recalls the encounter with Stein rather less charitably. After the two struck up a dinner conversation, he reports that

> in some way or other we got on to the subject of art. I believe it started by my admiring the view from the dining-room window. But Gertrude showed little enthusiasm. "Nature," she said, "is commonplace; imitation is more interesting." She enlarged on this thesis, stating that imitation marble looked more beautiful than the real thing, and that a Turner sunset was lovelier than any real sky. Although these pronouncements were rather derivative, I politely agreed with her.
>
> She theorized about cinema plots: "They are too hackneyed, complicated and contrived." She would like to see me in a movie just walking up the street and turning a corner, then another corner, and another. I thought of saying that her idea was a paraphrase of that mystic emphasis of hers: "Rose is a rose is a rose"—but an instinct stopped me.[36]

Chaplin seems to scoff at Stein as a pseudointellectual, one who speaks glibly and beyond what he considered her limited knowledge of art. As a result, he finds her remarks trite and her pose off-putting. It is hardly the meeting of minds suggested in Stein's version.

Perhaps it was this dismissive tone toward the writer in Chaplin's *Autobiography* that made Toklas, always protective of Stein, issue what is effectively a written retraction of the earlier compliment to Chaplin. His harsh appraisal of Stein effectively conjures the double bind she experienced when attempting alliances between high culture and mass culture; Chaplin deemed her views as too contrived to be commercially viable, too simple to be artistically important. She was left serving neither God nor Mammon, addressing neither elite nor popular audiences. Chaplin's derisive approach to Stein must have stung the woman who at that point lived as widow to her genius. At the same time, Chaplin's judgments echo the sentiments of many of Stein's detractors, particularly concerning her relationship to popular forms.

Although an expatriate writing chiefly in France, then, Stein was no means a stranger to an emerging American mass culture. By her own testimony, both in published works and correspondence, Stein had extremely eclectic cultural tastes, even as a reader. For this reason, critic Ann Douglas refers to Stein as "a devotee of what might be called the uncritical mass."[37] In this respect, Stein resembles Virginia Woolf, whom critic Angela Hewett laments "reserved time for what she called (unfortunately, without irony) her 'trash' or 'rubbish' reading, and she was both familiar with and often was delighted (if not inspired) by the picture palaces, music hall performances, department stores, advertisements, bestsellers, and mass-produced goods (particularly cars and car fashions) of the postwar period."[38] While living and working in Paris, Stein sometimes had to take extraordinary measures to gratify these tastes, as when she implored friends to go to drugstores and train stations in the United States to supply her with mysteries. Some failed her by deeming these requests facetious, leaving her to insist, as she once did in a letter to Carl Van Vechten, "but I like novels bad novels, poor novels, detective novels, sentimental novels."[39] It is easy to fault Stein for her omnivorous tastes, but who is to say it was enthusiasm untempered with irony? It is difficult, perhaps impossible, to prove the absence of a tongue-in-cheek pleasure behind Stein's appetite for popular texts.

It was not unusual for modernist writers to address themselves to mass culture. "After all," writes theorist Andreas Huyssen, "both modernism and the avantgarde always defined their identity in relation to two cultural phenomena: traditional bourgeois high culture (especially the traditions of romantic idealism and of enlightened realism and representation), but also vernacular and popular culture as it was increasingly transformed into modern commercial mass culture."[40] It was simply more unusual for high modernist writers to do other than revile mass-cultural forms. To be sure, some women modernists—such as Virginia Woolf, Nella Larsen, and Rebecca West—bespoke an ambivalent relationship to mass culture and its make-believe world for women. As

Ellen Berry notes in *Curved Thought and Textual Wandering,* however, Stein took a distinctive approach to the relationship between modernism and mass culture.

> Unlike many modernist writers, Stein did not participate in the modernist repudiation of mass culture, did not insist on a rigid distinction between those two cultural spheres. Rather, in much of her work she embraced postmodern assumptions about art and culture, an aesthetic orientation growing out of her recognition that an early-twentieth-century moment represented a rapidly changing cultural situation, one in which an emerging mass culture played a central role. Recognizing the inescapability of mass culture in any effort to account for contemporary reality, and fascinated by it, Stein attempted to merge high art with certain forms and genres of mass culture and the culture of everyday life, self-consciously mixing these popular modes with avant-garde discourses in order to undermine the premises of realism. Thus Stein's texts not only anticipate many of the forms and logics widely evident in postmodern cultural practices; they also represent one of the first attempts to articulate the modern *through* the popular rather than in reaction to it.[41]

Stein found through popular culture a vehicle by which women might occupy different roles, even if that role play was fraught with identifications with the working- and middle-class commodities of consumer culture. For while "the bourgeoisie consolidated itself as respectable and conventional body by withdrawing itself from the popular, it constructed the popular as grotesque otherness," those who knew all too well the role of grotesque other could not fall so easily into the trap.[42] Stein could not simply reject popular culture as something beneath her station. She knew that she was an outsider to respectability and conventionality. To judge mass culture too harshly would be tantamount to self-loathing.

Those who, like Stein, ventured to experiment during the 1920s and 1930s with mass-cultural forms helped to reconfigure "respectable" writing genres, including many of the definitive genres of postmodernism. Douglas writes of such innovators,

> Their work whatever its artistic merits (and they were usually high), had historic importance in forming the genres that still dominate mass culture today: the *New Yorker* "casual," the syndicated editorial page, the gossip column, the smart urban comedy for stage and screen, the gangster movie, the talk show, the ad layout, the continuity comic

strip, the hit-single record, the sexually explicit novel, and the packaged public persona of mass celebrities whether sports heroes, actors, literary stars, or politicians. (Douglas, 127)

Douglas goes on to specify that "Stein loved the effortlessness and abundance created by the new technology of consumer-oriented mass production and saw her own art as its ally and analogue" (Douglas, 127). The essence of paradox is that a statement may be true at the precise time that its converse may also be true. If Stein saw her work as "ally and analogue" to mass culture, she seems also to have approached this alliance as a sharp-tongued friend.

"Being One Finding": Detective Fiction

> Anything is a detective story if it can be found out and can anything be found out.
>
> —Gertrude Stein

Stein's enthusiasms for popular forms were many and varied. Perhaps the most conspicuous of her interests in mass culture, given her reputation as an avant-garde writer, would be her affection for popular genre literature. Her tastes as a reader were, to say the least, eclectic. Since childhood, she had devoured books of every sort; indeed, she despaired when she realized that in one lifetime she would not succeed in reading everything that had been written. She consoled herself by reading as much as she could, including the *Congressional Record*. As a literary omnivore, she had an appetite for the written word in all its forms; all were "real" to her (*ABT*, 74–75). That is not to say that she did not enjoy favorites among her readings. She professed a true fondness for dime novels and pulp fiction. She took pleasure in Westerns and detective novels, and during her Paris years she begged correspondents to send her mystery stories from drugstores in the States. Each was a treasure to her and "no one must make fun of it" (*ABT*, 75).

Therefore, while Stein clearly took note of the literary tradition, as her autobiographical narratives attest, she also regarded closely the developments in popular fiction. She did not presume the inferiority of the formulas associated with popular genres, such as detective stories. Rather, she deemed these living forms, more reflective of modern writing than many of their upscale counterparts.

This chapter focuses on Stein's keen and reasonably far-reaching interest in discourse concerning crime, police work, concealment, and detection. Although this fascination may be best known through Stein's mystery novella, *Blood on the Dining-Room Floor*, a number of other Stein texts also find her invoking and commenting on the genre, its narrative modes, and its distinctive appeal to audiences. For this reason, in addition to examining *Blood on the Dining-Room Floor*, this chapter also discusses more generally the value Stein attached to detective stories and her rationale for doing so. Other texts relevant to this purpose include Stein's "Subject-Cases: The Background of a Detective Story," "Reflections on the Atomic Bomb," "American Crimes and How They Matter," *The Geographical History of America*, and her so-called autobiographical writings, in which she comments on her preoccupation with popular literature narratives and forms, particularly the detective story.

One of the features of detective stories that Stein enjoyed the most was the narrative sequence particular to the murder mystery. As a writer who worked against a linear progression of time and plot within her own texts, Stein found refreshingly modern the devices of murder mysteries, in which the victim (whom Stein regarded as the genre's true hero, even though often a stranger both to characters and readers) is already dead by the moment the reader begins the story. With characteristic irreverence, Stein declares her belief that "novels are therefore not very good these days unless they are detective stories" (*EA*, 123). In other words, since stories of murder begin with an ending, Stein finds them freeing to the writer in terms of textual construction. She need not restrict herself to linear time. Her text could begin with an ending, a death.

From stylistic formulas, plots, form, and methods of characterization to pieties of content, Stein set out to commit a symbolic murder of the past, and with it her literary forebears. In this sense, the struggle to read Stein's work resembles the work conducted by the reader of a murder mystery. The question is not so much "whodunit," as it is how, why, and with what result. In an important sense, Stein's innovations take place "over the dead bodies" of her literary predecessors. Her writings position her as both the culprit and the sleuth as she narrates this necessary crime.

As Nathalie Clifford Barney once wrote of Stein's "Subject-Cases: The Background of a Detective Story," "if the best detective story is the one whose mystery remains complete and the crime undiscovered, this one should win!" (*AFAM*, xviii). As an elusive writer, Stein was always one to give chase. Readers continue to pursue her words across pages, seeking clues and solutions to her mysterious texts. It makes sense, then, that she was endlessly fascinated by crime and detective stories, both fictional and nonfictional. The American lecture tour found her following the case of John Dillinger, taking a ride-along with Chicago's homicide squad, and meeting one of her favorite mystery writers, Dashiell Hammett. In fact, Stein's friend Bennett Cerf reports in *Try and Stop Me* that "Gertrude said that she was replacing Dillinger as the sensation of the moment."[43] Writing *Blood on the Dining-Room Floor* gave

Stein the opportunity to bring together these interests from life and fiction. Stein critics have taken due notice of the writer's professed affinity for detective fiction. Portions of book-length studies by Harriet Chessman, Alison Rieke, and Richard Kostelanetz comment on the novella in this context.[44] In addition, a variety of articles or short pieces by such critics as Brooks Landon, Susanne Rohr, and Jane Detweiler focuses specifically on *Blood on the Dining-Room Floor* as a narrative of mystery and detection.[45] This scholarship has tended to focus on what the text has in common with detective novels. It may be as important to consider those ways in which Stein's text breaks away.

The form of narrative address in *Blood on the Dining-Room Floor* suggests a story told aloud, to a scribe or other listener, whom the narrator commonly speaks to by name as Lizzie. The speaking voice in the novella punctuates her tale with asides to Lizzie. These remarks seem mostly designed to ensure that Lizzie is listening, understands what is being said, and follows the story as it develops. It is not clear whether this textual guidance is provided because the story is difficult or because the reader is.

There are also references to a wider audience, about whom the narrator has similar concerns of understanding. The text sporadically poses questions or furnishes directions to its readers. The narrator purports to call the reader's attention to true clues and appears at some pains to guide the reader through matters of consequence in the story.

In terms of a plot, *Blood on the Dining-Room Floor* seems to be a multi-layered detective text, with cases heaped upon unrelated cases. The narrator appears to enjoy these layers, but the listener warns against their potential to confuse readers. Stein writes, "How often could I add so many cases to as many more. But she said if I add will anybody hover as they do hover from cover to cover" (*BDR*, 61). As with the dialogue with an auditor, this comment shows the narrator struggling with two competing impulses. On one hand, the narrator wants to indulge her own taste for textual complication. In this sense, the narrator makes an effort to defend the text's eccentricities, indicating "there had to be breaking up of families and killing of dogs and spoiling of sons and losing of daughters and killing of mothers and banishing of fathers" (*BDR*, 51). On the other hand, the narrator wants to bring readers along through the text's labyrinth, so she must temper the effects of these complications with words of help and reassurance. For this reason, the narrator seems regularly to implore the audience to listen carefully and "Read while I write" (*BDR*, 77).

The proliferation of plots and details seems sufficient to threaten basic understanding of the detective story, for both listener and narrator. At one point, Stein writes, "Can you see crime. No not I" (*BDR*, 49). Even periodic efforts to sum up the story structure seem ill-fated: "So now you see. We have the triple theme" (*BDR*, 62–63). Even the novella's chapter lengths seem to reflect the strained effort to make the text intelligible, as when chapter 16 consists of just 13 words arranged in the form of a question. When the narrative becomes mired, the speaker asks "Has everybody got it straight" (*BDR*, 26), wonders "Do you remember" (*BDR*, 35), and advises the audience to "Read the beginning again" (*BDR*, 26).

There are several mysteries buried within the text, things even the narrator owns "nobody can know" (*BDR*, 28). There is talk of people being sent off or put away. There are lurid suggestions of conspiratorial romances. There is the country house, where a woman falls to her death inexplicably in the night. There are the disgruntled or devious servants who appear to have tampered with the telephone and automobiles. There are three young women who make unfortunate marriages. There is a horticultural garden and its suspicious caretakers. There are bold hints of guilt as well as protestations of innocence. These stories twine through the novella without clear connection to each other or narrative resolution at the end. It is as if we, as readers, must sift through seemingly unrelated bits to construct an explanation as would be usual in crime fiction. "A fact is not surprising," writes Stein, "a coincidence is surprising and that is the reason that crime is surprising. There is always coincidence in crime" (*BDR*, 42). In this way, the reader searches out the interplay among these cases or subplots, hopeful that the coincidences will hold an explanatory power.

It is as if the story has gone into hiding along with the culprit, though, and the reader is left to guess what is important or telling about the text. The language of the text seems as concerned with what it conceals as it does with what it reveals, from start to finish. Therefore, Stein challenges even the customs of the detective genre. If, as Susannah Radstone maintains, "Traditional detective fiction is a highly formalized and predictable genre offering pleasure and release of tension through the affirmation of received and uncontested meanings,"[46] then Stein confounds the genre of detective stories by refusing the reader affirmation of expected meaning. She places all facts and forms in question. Of *Blood on the Dining-Room Floor*, Michael Hoffman posits that "The major interest is not linguistic but generic; it lies in watching Stein take a traditional, ritualistic form like the detective story and violate almost all of its conventions while still maintaining somehow the basic tone and concerns familiar to it. Although it is like no other detective story, it quite definitively points out by its irreverence the artificiality of many of the 'whodunit's' conventional concerns."[47] As she does with other vernacular writing forms, Stein appropriates what she prizes about the genre, discards what she does not, and fashions from this material a new hybrid—a text fulfilling the expectations of neither high literature nor popular fiction.

For this reason, although quite taken with the form, Stein abandons the most central and cherished convention of the detective genre, the text's dramatic movement toward solution. In this regard, Bettina Knapp writes of Stein, "her flagrant distrust of the artificiality and superficiality of literary genres led her to deconstruct the villain, the hero, and the pseudoreading of the detective. Her conclusion for *Blood on the Dining-Room Floor*—in rhyme, no less—was 'And now, he had been there, where the lady fell, very well.' And what of Stein's reaction to the death of Mme. Pernollet, ostensibly her friend? Detached and unfeeling. Nor did her demise really matter since 'no one is amiss after servants are changed. Are they.' "[48] The story's last page loops back to the first, where the reader first learned about the circumstances that precipitated the initial change in servants. Consequently, the reader is left to reread the beginning and reenter the story to complete the text. This circular movement spins away from fiction's usually linear progression of events and their telling.

Stein's own pose within her experiments in detective and crime fiction seems to linger with the wrongdoer as much as with the sleuth. There is a sense in which Stein's writing, here and elsewhere, characterizes her as a transgressor or criminal. Whether due to the backlash against her disclosures and postures in *The Autobiography of Alice B. Toklas* or for other reasons, she refers in her writing to the "motive" and to "Witnesses of my autobiography" (*GHA*, 88). By opening up her life and those of others in the mode of autobiography, Stein saw herself as both reporting and committing a crime. On counts literary and social, she risks being "found out." At the same time, she seems to inform on herself, perhaps to establish that "identity has nothing to do with crime. With the detective story but not with crime" (*GHA*, 144). Through her refiguring of this writing genre, she announces the ways in which she is implicated by both literary and cultural suspicion.

That Stein would find in popular forms such as the detective story a vehicle for exploring her life as a suspect, in terms of both her writing and personal lives, suggests one reason why her text cannot include a solution or ending. Stein herself had none. The course of her career is itself a story of Stein's ceaseless efforts to situate herself in a world no better prepared to accept her words than it was to accept her ways. Therefore, Stein's texts inscribe this tension between expression and explanation, as when she called *The Geographical History of America* "a detective story of how to write" (*GHA*, 120). Similarly, Harriet Chessman has described *Blood on the Dining-Room Floor* as a parable of reading and detection in which the reader's movement through the text forms a metanarrative.

If Stein's *Blood on the Dining-Room Floor* is a metanarrative about reading and constructing meaning with the text of her novella, it simultaneously offers a subtextual narrative about reading the lives of others. Rather than a depiction of creative coexistence, the text portrays an atmosphere of scrutiny and suspicion, where much—sometimes too much—is made of people's differences as cause for alarm. Given the ways—social, sexual, and textual—Stein herself is decidedly different, the narrator's voice in *Blood on the Dining-Room Floor* seems to speak with irony on several levels, when asking the story's readers, "Has everybody got it straight"? In more ways than one, Stein was not a straight writer and did not aspire to be. With its ambience of secrecy and mystery, *Blood on the Dining-Room Floor* points to a need for new stories of discovery, in which one's human or literary differences, even if found out, would not incriminate.

"Being a Young One": Children's Fiction

> What do you tell and how do you tell it.
>
> —Gertrude Stein

In 1992, a statue of Gertrude Stein was placed on public display in New York's Bryant Park, located just behind the Public Library.[49] Along with a tribute to Eleanor Roosevelt, dedicated in the same year, the Stein memorial represents the first commemorative sculpture of an American woman in the history of New York City. Prior to that time, the closest New York had come to dedicating monuments to recognize the contributions of women was to present statues of two fictional females: Mother Goose and Alice in Wonderland. Even though she had been derided as the "Mother Goose of Montparnasse," and despite the fact that she attributed her favorite meditation on identity, "I am I because my little dog knows me," to Mother Goose, Stein might appear, at first glance, to offer strange company to these icons of children's literature (*EA*, 297). Indeed, given Stein's reputation as a literary heretic, many readers are stunned to learn that Stein wrote and published two titles for children, *The World Is Round* and *Alphabets and Birthdays*.[50] Both books are, to say the least, irregular for the genre of juvenile literature. This chapter examines the nature and implications of Stein's forays into children's fiction, particularly with *The World Is Round*. At the same time that these texts show Stein playing with the narrative conventions of children's stories (song, superstition, parable, naming, storytelling), she takes her own characteristic liberties with plot, characterization, syntax, and subject matter as they are typically encountered in children's literature. At the same time that Stein's writings for children mobilize formulas of playful perception familiar among stories for children, they also refuse those formulas in ways that are as unmistakable as they are irreverant. Viewed as a response to the configuration of what folklorists call the European magic tale, Stein's writings for children, through their appropriation of conventional writing forms, pit mother wit against master narratives of male quest, heroism, and authoritative speech.

It is hard to elude the fact that retro escapism is the order of the popular culture day. From motion pictures such as *Batman, Dick Tracy,* and *Hook,* to Broadway's productions of *Annie* and *Into the Woods,* to cable television's *Faerie Tale Theatre* and *Nick at Nite,* to soaring profits in rental and purchase of other new and reissued children's video fare, it seems clear that Americans are paying big bucks to feel little once more. Indeed, American onlookers have a difficult time imagining why EuroDisney, an American-style-in-Paris theme park, might not be prospering as expected.[51] Meanwhile, the American nostalgia industry thrives, especially when a return to childhood's "wonder year" narratives finds us feeling wiser to (and/or wiser than) the tales being told.

Contemporary America's enterprising/merchandizing embrace of such stories as *Beauty and the Beast* and *The Little Mermaid* suggests that some readers (perhaps those commonly identified as baby boomers) feel particular nostalgia for the Disneyfied animated narratives they remember. Their devotion to such traditional tales may correspond to a wish to reaffirm—now through viewing with their own children—what are by now almost euphemistically referred to as family values. Even in the realm of imaginary characters, it is easier for some to respond to Charlie Brown than Murphy Brown.

But not all of these contemporary versions of traditional tales aspire to faithful renditions of the "original" cultural text. For some, it is estrangement as much as enchantment that compels both writers and readers to revisit stories associated with youth. For these individuals, the time has come to talk back.[52]

It is hardly new for disenfranchised writers, women writers for example, to return to childhood's stories for an empowering second look and retort. The stakes remain high in the contest over the influence children's tales exert over their readers. For example, Marcia Lieberman, in her article " 'Some Day My Prince Will Come': Female Acculturation Through the Fairy Tale," maintains that childhood stories function as important ideological scripts for readers' lives: "Not only do children find out what happens to the various princes and princesses, woodcutters, witches, and children of their favorite tales, but they also learn behavioral and associational patterns, value systems, and how to predict the consequences of specific acts or circumstances."[53] If these tales have spoken to us, what have we now to say back to them? What remains to be said? In other words, what stories do readers of fairy tales and fables tell?

Over the years, some readers have talked back to these familiar tales by seeking to resituate their narrative sequences. In her image-word text, "Mirror Mirror" (1986–1987), for example, artist Carrie Mae Weems engages in some back talk concerning the racial politics of children's stories such as "Snow White." Beneath a photograph of an African American woman casting her own gaze away from a mirror in which the viewer finds reflected the image of a white fairy princess, one reads the caption: "LOOKING INTO THE MIRROR, THE BLACK WOMAN ASKED, 'MIRROR MIRROR ON THE WALL, WHO'S THE FINEST OF THEM ALL?' THE MIRROR SAYS, 'SNOW WHITE, YOU BLACK BITCH, AND DON'T YOU FORGET IT!!!' "[54] In the "classic" tale of Snow White, a woman stands poised and hopeful before a mirror, awaiting its verdict of her desirability relative to other women. The mirror is not the instrument of her vision but rather an apparatus for her appraisal and control by others. What she "sees" in the looking glass is her rank, her beauty caste (fair, fairer, fairest). As Weems makes vivid in her image-word text, there is no recognition for difference or for racial pigment that is other than "snow white.' The woman in this photograph learns to fear the image waiting in the mirror. A woman is called vain if she likes what she sees in the mirror, compromised if she turns away.

It is the distortions of such mirrors, looking glasses that seek to replace women's perceptions with white male standards, that prompted Mary Daly to characterize America as a "Looking Glass Society," which she defines as follows:

> 1: patriarchy: the house of mirrors, the world of reversals 2: the society in which women serve as magnifying mirrors reflecting men at twice their natural size 3: society manufactured by phallocrats, who project their own deficiencies upon all Others, attempting to convert these into reflections of their own inadequate selves.[55]

It is a mirror that casts an image rather than reflect one's own. The chief horror in this not-so-fun house of mirrors is that women will believe what others' mirrors tell them, especially about who they are. They may feel pressure to become what they see there. With her alternative approach to the narrative formula of "Snow White," Carrie Mae Weems shows it in a different light.

Toni Cade Bambara's anthology, *Tales and Stories for Black Folk*, is another such example of back talk to children's narratives as ideological scripts for a "looking glass society."[56] Featured in this volume are such re-visioned tales as "Chicken Licken" and "The Three Little Pigs." Bambara and her student writers not only modernize the contextual references within these stories, they also offer a kind of political critique and corrective to them.

Take, for instance, the familiar story of the three little pigs. In the hands of Geneva Powell and Toni Cade Bambara, this children's story is transformed into "The Three Little Panthers" (Bambara, 140–41). With this new version, the Panthers integrate "the forest called the suburbs." Their presence is greeted with cross burnings and cries that, "IF YOU DON'T MOVE, I'LL HUFF AND I'LL PUFF AND I'LL BLOW YOUR HOUSE UP." After eventually winning the acceptance of the other animals in the suburbs, the Panthers realize that they are not accepted on their own terms. From their new neighbors, the Panthers have received gifts that exact a price. Written on the gift cards is the message: "YOU DON'T HAVE TO MOVE. WE REALLY LIKE YOU PEOPLE. BUT YOU DON'T EAT PROPERLY. YOU DRESS FUNNY. AND YOUR I. Q. IS LOW. SO PLEASE USE OUR GIFTS SO YOU CAN BE LIKE US. AND WE WON'T HUFF AND PUFF." The neighbors have held up a mirror to the Panthers and asked them to conform. It is but another mirror that casts an image rather than reflects one's own, and so the Panthers go "back home where they could be loved and be for real." The changes to the story are more than cosmetic, then; they are fundamental revisions of plot. They are also affirmations of autonomous identity ("for real" and not for show) and autonomous narrative (a story of one's own).

In this respect, Stein herself was nothing if not a genre rebel, working within and across writing forms from detective fiction to erotic poetry, autobiography to opera, word portraits to Faustian drama. It should surprise no one to learn that Stein also published writing directed to children, perhaps most notably *The World Is Round,* an innovative response to the formulas of spiritual narrative and the European magic tale.[57] By taking up a few crucial scenes from Gertrude Stein's *The World Is Round,* it is possible to explore the sense in which this text de-code-ifies master narratives of male quest, spiritual expression, and authoritative speech.

Little has been written about Gertrude Stein's *The World Is Round.* Yet embedded within that story is a narrative so captivating (and captive, fugitive) as to insist on our notice. I refer to chapters 13 through 34, which stand as a counterstatement within the text—in both senses, then, forming the work's subtext. It is the story of a little girl named Rose and her journey heavenward (better to see). It is the story of a writer in her sixties, still negotiating her literary ascent (better to be seen). It is the story of the woman visionary. It is the fashioning of woman lore, at times possible only by breaking the cake of androcentric custom.[58]

Nevertheless, when critics read this text, even their summaries of it betray conventional (rather than experimental) readings. In large part, they deform the text to accomodate their own narrative expectations for children's stories, particularly in terms of endings. Here is Bruce Kellner's synopsis of *The World Is Round*:

> Rose sings a good deal and plays with her cousin Willie. He sings as well, and Rose cries a lot. They become involved with some wild animals, notably a lion named Billie. This shorter, first adventure in *The World Is Round* is less interesting than the second one, in which Rose carries a blue chair up a mountain. The journey is fraught with the perils of an epic for the nursery. There is a great deal of thinking about the trip, ruminating on the passing of time through the cycle of day and night, the deliberation, her fear of the dark, and her bravery. . . . Then bells ring, the mountain rises above the green grass meadow, and finally Rose reaches the top, sits down in her chair, and sings a number of songs. That night a searchlight from a neighboring mountaintop spots her, Willie at the controls. They turn out not to be cousins after all, get married, and live happily every after.[59]

Day after day, line by line, we demonstrate that as readers, we re-tell stories as we read them. We recast them in the images available to us—creating the story in a form of collaborative activity.

Stein's *The World Is Round* asserts that this narrative impulse, particularly toward autobiography, is a compelling one, uniting all creatures. All like to tell stories. Rose not only liked to tell, she also liked telling others what to do. Early on in the tale, it also becomes clear that storytellers are accorded a measure of liberty and authority in the culture. Rose's cousin Willie invokes this power as he reprises the formulaic opening line of children's narrative ("Once upon a time") and, during the telling of his own story, observes "I do as I please / Run around the world just as I please. / I Willie" (*WIR*, 29). Willie does as he wishes, and his entitlement to run around the world recalls the story's name. With its very title, Stein's narrative establishes an environment of emphatically preferred perceptions. This story, like most, begins with placement of belief (here registered as the cultural predicate that the earth, and motions on it, are continuous, regular, and cyclical): "Once upon a time the world was round and you could go on it around and around" (*WIR*, 7). In a round world, motion (if not e-motion) is predictable and comfortingly recurrent. This axial spin holds the earth and its inhabitants in eternal balance (or inexorable tension). The chief benefit of this schema is continuity. Like the familiar tag line of children's narrative, "Once upon a time" (which in successive tellings comes to stand for every time), then, this view ("the world is round") forms the foundation for human experiences and their telling.

This is the authorized version of reality, the one through which education carries Rose, like a dense forest of comforting and sustaining fictions. This regulating worldview forms a protective screen from the unexpected and untoward, and like "the woods [it serves as] the poor man's overcoat, and it is true there in the woods no rain comes through no sun comes through no snow comes through no dust comes through, there has to be a lot of anything before in a thick wood it does come through" (*WIR*, 89). Little impinges on the dwellers of this forest haven, except perhaps the occasional doubt.

Rose, however, finds herself with more than the occasional misgiving about this utopia of round worlds and rose-colored perceptions. "I am Rose," she explains, "but I am not rosy" (*WIR*, 111). As she reflects on school lessons that render all matters and their outcomes regular, Rose does more than wonder about the unspoken portion of this preferred narrative. The text's speaking voice indicates of Rose that

> The teacher taught her
> That the world was round
> That the sun was round
> That the moon was round
> That the stars were round
> And that they were all going around and around
> And not a sound.
>
> (*WIR*, 22)

What hadn't the teacher taught her? What possibilities remained unuttered (without "a sound")? Rose becomes suspicious of this story with its happy and uniform endings, deciding that she does not believe it. Rather than a comfort, then, others' refrains of the world's roundness only recall to Rose the companion claims of the inexorable cycle of time and the inevitable repetition of its movements. This master narrative of a perfect and perfectly round world leaves Rose wondering if any force might break the pattern of its revolutions, to intervene in the world's seemingly unstoppable direction.

Others, with their claims of the world's roundness, do more than disturb Rose's reverie, then; they make her pleasures and discoveries impossible. "Once someone told her that the stars were round and she wished that they had not told her" (*WIR*, 19). Their tale makes hers untellable. If she listens to those stories that others (teachers and other "someones") tell, she can only retell their tales. If she retells theirs, she will never tell her own.

Her story is one that needs to be told, though, if only because it is unorthodox. If there is one thing readers learn about Rose, it is that she is no conventional girl. That is, Stein goes to some lengths to establish this figure as gender-transgressive. Make no mistake; Rose "carries a pen-knife" and "had nothing pink" (*WIR*, 91). Emancipated from gender role-playing, Rose may devote herself to alternative plans of action. In this regard, Rose seems to be engaged in constant, ongoing activity. She climbs, decides, makes noise. Far from the passive, appreciative sidekick or helpmate in male adventure narratives, "Rose had courage everywhere" and she makes her journey alone (*WIR*, 102).

To disrupt the narrative (and worldly) sequence, with its insistence on roundness, therefore, Rose looks up to the mountains. With this in mind, she resolves to carry a blue chair up a mountain and sit at its summit. As with most such tales, however, this story is more about the journey than its destination. What she sees, does, and reckons along the way make all the difference—or at least they could. Many of her visions, deeds, and inferences involve or invert existing narrative traditions: song, superstition, parable, naming, and storytelling. Stein's is a reverse, a fairy tale that talks back to these traditions. At the same time that *The World Is Round* mobilizes formulas of playful perception familiar among stories for children, it also refuses those formulas in ways that are as unmistakable as they are irreverent.

By contesting social meanings (Must the world be round?), Rose rather literally puts her own spin on the earth's rotation. As a spinster/creatrix, she reinvents the world on her own terms, turns it on her own axis, then heads to the hilltops to survey the results. Here I borrow Mary Daly's definition:

> Spinning 1: Gyn/Ecological creation; Discovering the lost thread of connectedness within the cosmos and repairing this thread in the

process; whirling and twirling the threads of Life on the axis of Spinsters' own being 2: turning quickly on one's heel; moving counter-
clockwise; whirling away in all directions from the death march of
patriarchy. (Daly, 96)

As she climbs, Rose leaves her daily world behind and takes on a newly
passionate relationship to nature, of which she ("Rose") is a part. She
discovers feelings and longings that are so unfamiliar to her that at
times they seem inexpressible; that is, she feels "funny" quite a lot
(*WIR*, 70). As she rises, she calls into question each bit of conventional
wisdom, modifying it in such a way as to satisfy her own sensibilities.

Rose looks to songs to help her survive and celebrate her accomplish-
ments. In the face of the teacher's claims of a round world, she sings. In
fact, as Rose resolves to climb the mountain with her blue chair, she
raises her voice in song even before raising a foot to climb. It is a love
song of sorts to the natural wonder before her. Humbled and attracted
by the landform's majesty, Rose literally sings its praises. She makes a
tearful vow to reach the summit. Her use of the word "will" here has a
triple meaning insofar as with the pledge she is also composing an ode
to volition ("I will"), and taking for herself the male prerogative of
cousin Willie ("I will"). After reaching the mountaintop, she sings once
more, again of will: "*Will you* sang Rose *oh yes you will*. And she sang *oh Will
oh Will* and she cried and cried and cried and cried and the search light
went round and round and round and round" (*WIR*, 116; italics added).

Critics have tended to see Rose's journey up the mountain within the
interpretive framework of a male adventure or quest narrative. As
recently as 1988, Bruce Kellner characterized the story as "an epic for
the nursery" (Kellner, 69). There is at least one other way to read Rose's
journey, though—not as a trip for sport or glory but rather as a planned
escape. After all, consider the way Rose's ascent disrupts the narrative
surface and sequence of the text, thereby placing Rose at its entitled
center. Recall, too, the details of her departure. She "left early so no one
saw her," suggesting that secrecy is a feature of her plan (*WIR*, 66). Her
approach to the "stay away' journey is anything but casual; in fact, she
takes furniture with her. It seems no coincidence here that she takes
the object of furniture also associated with lion taming. Once atop the
mountain, she mounts her chair/throne and recounts her escape in song,
for once telling her own tale, saying that, "Once upon a time there was
a way to stay to stay away" (*WIR*, 111–12). Rose conquers her fears in
order to reach the summit, only to be found there by ringing bells and a

searchlight piercing the night's cover of darkness. A sentence later, Rose is married to Willie, raising children, and returned to a very round world.

A sentence in a story doubles as the sentence for Rose's transgression and escape. She must be reabsorbed into society at any cost. Therefore, the final chapter, fittingly marked as "The End," reveals that Rose and Willie are not related after all, a plot turn so inexplicable that even the text concedes "just how nobody knows" (*WIR*, 117). There is no easy way to recover the narrative that began the text, but one matter is certain: the tale cannot end with a victorious and enthroned woman bathed in light. Here rests the difference between an end and an ending, between form and formula. Just as critic Rachel Blau DuPlessis writes of the power of literary endings to constrain women's destinies and contain their transgressions, for the sake of story closure, the wild Rose must be tamed.[60]

It is similarly remarkable how readily critics have adopted a rationalization of the light Rose experiences on the hilltop. They seem altogether prepared to attribute this light to Willie's agency. As Kellner writes matter-of-factly of this scene, "That night a searchlight from a neighboring mountaintop spots her, Willie at the controls" (Kellner, 69). Richard Bridgman goes so far as to say that Rose's "relief comes in the form of light. A search-light, operated by her cousin from another mountain, sweeps all around Rose, brightening the sky and ground."[61] It appears, however, a speculation of the moment, as much as anything else, that the light Rose sees has its source in "Will" (whom these critics equate with Willie). This tendency to award gender roles of agency to Willie and receptivity to Rose proves problematic throughout Bridgman's reading of *The World Is Round.* That is to say, those same characteristics that mark Willie as "expeditious" and "an adventurous boy" discredit Rose as "a rather willful, disturbed girl." Bridgman portrays Rose as "weeping," "oppressed," in "mental crisis," perhaps engaged in "corrective therapy" and "more depressed than she is actually threatened" (Bridgman, 45, 300, 299, 304, 302, 303) This therapeutic version of Rose fails to show her path as logical, instead preferring to find her pathological. In Bridgman's account, she sounds neurasthenic. The source of the light Rose sees remains unidentified, whether earthly or divine. The illumination has elements of both epiphany and apocalypse, as the tale struggles toward a resolution of its narrative action.

In this sense, Stein's (and Rose's) story is a non sequitur, arriving at an outcome not indicated by sequential logic. For a while, though, the story belongs to Rose. When "she did not have any ink," she used her penknife to carve her name in rings around a tree trunk (*WIR*, 91). This ring of roses becomes her inscription, her presence on the narrative landscape. If, as Mary Daly maintains, a patriarchy is constructed and maintained through "the numbing/dumbing of potential spell-speakers through enforced rote memorizing and reciting of patriarchal reversals, as in sexist nursery rhymes, patriarchal poetry, 'history' lessons, bible/babble lessons," then Rose, however briefly, rises above it through her physical and narrative acts (Daly, 248).

In her efforts to read and re-verse her environment and its web of social relations, Rose has engaged in a process of reeducation, first accomplished by questioning, then flight, and finally by unlearning the ways of the round world. As a young child, Rose had been taught stock answers. Now that she has scaled the mountain, she poses questions. She has come into her own voice. Once when she spoke before the mirror, she saw herself speaking in circles:

> She remembered when she had been young
> That one day she had sung,
> And there was a looking-glass in front of her
> And as she sang her mouth was round and was
> going around and around.
>
> (*WIR*, 22)

As Rose pursues her own vision and her own story, though, she shatters the looking glass (and with it, the formulaic narratives of a looking glass society). Beyond the mirror, she recovers wonder. Although this time the story may, ultimately, through narrative insistence, reabsorb Rose in the conventionality of the marriage plot, readers can experience this fate as an absurd concession to and reminder of the performance of gender demanded heretofore by popular fiction, with its ideological scripts that render female characters accountable to compulsory heterosexuality, romance, and the confines of wedlock. Stein must look further, and perhaps to other popular forms, if she is to find or fashion a key to unlock Rose from this state of captivity.

"Being Gay Ones": Erotic Fiction

> Literature—creative literature—unconcerned with sex is
> inconceivable.
>
> —Gertrude Stein

As reported in "How to Write Like Gertrude Stein," college composition teacher Philip Keith uses Gertrude Stein's texts in the classroom to reveal the limitations of what he considers to be the equation of writing instruction with mastery of language devices. In one such exercise, Keith's upper-level students tested E. D. Hirsch's principles (as expressed in *The Philosophy of Composition*) by using them to edit Stein. One example proves particularly illuminating. Here is a passage from Stein's "Forensics" in *How to Write*:

> Will he ask them why she chose this. If they do he will be disappointed in her being so withdrawn and reminded and when will two meet one. The necessity. Further. Should hurry be advantageous more in coming than in going in adding and following. Should he be they worship welling. Their emotion welled up but admittedly they were admiring.

And now, with a little help from Hirsch, Keith's student edits the same passage:

> Will he ask why? If so, she will withdraw and he will be disappointed they are no longer one. Necessity compels him to try. He wonders if rushing in will be advantageous, or if leaving the matter alone would be best. They would be worshipping each other, not sitting apart. Their emotion welled up as they eyed each other.[62]

Clearly this student's work, as far as it goes, does not edit so much as translate Stein. The means by which the student attempts to edit Stein will not prove surprising to any college teacher today. As Keith notes in his account of the classroom experiment, popular fiction sets the tone for the student's interventions in Stein's language. Western modes of logic and rhetoric, such as the if-then statement, structure the sentences, but mass-culture narratives shape the story. Invoking the heroic tales of rugged individualism embodied by male protagonists, the student repositions the male actor in a noble struggle ("Necessity compels him to try"). The dynamics of gender domination accompanying this formula of male heroism assign the female figure's role as reactive and ultimately submissive (if he asks why, "she will withdraw"). The action-imperative of popular writing makes introspection sound stilted and improbable ("He wonders if rushing in will be advantageous"), and all that the male and female figures in the passage seem to share is a measure of sentimentality and thinly disguised sexual desire befitting romance plots ("Their emotions welled up as they eyed each other"). The edited Stein passage has been rendered as a linear narrative and, not coincidentally, a literal reinscription of a culture's ideological scripts. In this case, the translation models come chiefly from mass-market erotic fiction.

After reaching this point in the Stein text, though, the student ceases what she has come to recognize as a "ridiculous task." The edited version is just one word shorter than Stein's, and yet it says considerably less. The principles by which the student has set out to order Stein's unruly text have not enabled her to "repair" the passage, only to replace it. The editing experiment is a failure, while Keith's lesson about reductive approaches to Stein is a success. Writing is not merely the imposition of grammatical rules and literary prototypes but a "resource for experience and thought." Although editors of her day complained that Stein wrote as if unaccustomed to the English language, Stein may have quite a bit to teach us about our own acts of reading, writing, and loving.

The focus within this chapter is on the narrative form at work in Stein erotic writings in prose, particularly as she engages and/or subverts the conventional representations of desire in literary romance and the love story. For this reason, particular attention is directed to a single text, Stein's "Didn't Nelly and Lilly Love You." This composition can be situated in the context of other relationship-based Stein texts, both prose and poetry, most of which were written during the early years of Stein's long-lived relationship with Alice B. Toklas, such as "Many Many Women" and "A Long Gay Book." *Q.E.D.*, Stein's first novel, serves as a point of comparison to "Didn't Nelly and Lilly Love You" within this discussion.

In writing about romantic fiction as form, literary critic Amal Treacher briefly outlines its narrative contours: "Contained within fiction, and articulated with unconscious desires and wishes, are longing, wanting, wishing to possess and to be possessed, erotic phantasies of passivity and activity, the need to be cherished and adored, being both powerful and powerless . . . the list is endless."[63] All of these desires and wishes course through Stein's textual romances. While a great many of Stein's writings contain sexual images and references, some of her works take romance as their primary subject. Critics sometimes refer to these works as Stein's erotica, most often noting the example of Stein's poem, "Lifting Belly."[64] "Lifting Belly," while frequently noted as exemplar of Stein's erotic writings, is but one of a number of such compositions from 1913 to 1919, such as "Possessive Case," "No," "Pink Melon Joy," "If You Had Three Husbands," "I Often Think About Another," "All Sunday," "The King or Something," and "The Present." Furthermore, although the period from 1913 to 1919 proved a most prolific time for Stein's erotic writing, she continued to write in this mode throughout her literary career. During the 1920s, she added to their number such noteworthy and related compositions as "A Sonatina Followed By Another," "As A Wife Has A Cow A Love Story," "Birth and Marriage," "A Book," "With a Wife," "A Third," and "A Lyrical Opera Made By Two To Be Sung."

In these works, Stein presents an antipatriarchal view of women's sexuality, particularly as expressed among women. That is to say, Stein celebrates sex, pronounces her pleasure in sex, declares her entitlement to write about sexual love among women, conducts her discussion of homosexual marriage, and pays tribute to that marriage by likening it to spiritual union. Love, as Stein represents it, is redemptive. These texts narrate a woman's desires, such as the longing of *Q.E.D.*'s Adele for a transcendent form of sexual love with another woman, one that might give her a feeling of completeness.

Some context for *Q.E.D.*, Stein's first novel, is helpful in this regard.[65] According to *The Autobiography of Alice B. Toklas*, it was not until 1932 that the manuscript came out of storage, where it had resided since Gertrude Stein had finished penning it in October 1903. Stein herself excluded this early novel from the Yale Catalogue.[66] She described it as "too outspoken for the times, even though it was restrained."[67] For a novel written in 1903, *Q.E.D.*'s treatment of lesbianism was unusually candid.

Adele functions as the primary character in the novel. She vies with Mabel for Helen's favor. *Q.E.D.* also chronicles Adele's exploration of the binary oppositions between mind and body, thought and feeling, reason and instinct, moral doctrine and moral conduct. Scholars have documented the parallels between *Q.E.D.*'s plot and events in Stein's life, as well as the parallels between this plot and plots for her subsequent writings, especially the "Melanctha" portion of *Three Lives*. One critic went so far as to describe *Q.E.D.* as a "purification ritual" for its author (Hobhouse, 31). Sensitive autobiographical material in *Q.E.D.* might have deterred Stein from publishing the novel. As Alice B. Toklas wrote of *Q.E.D.*, "the only thing I know is I wouldn't want it read—that is therefore not published—during my life. . . . Of course it must not be found here someday when Allan [Stein] comes and takes over."[68] Perhaps it was out of sympathy for Toklas that Stein kept *Q.E.D.* a secret.

Q.E.D. might have been particularly problematic on several counts. It has been claimed that Toklas objected to the novel's thinly disguised retelling of a love interest of Stein's predating the Toklas relationship. The correspondence between Gertrude Stein and May Bookstaver, one of the parties in that earlier romance, was sufficiently painful for Toklas to destroy the letters "in a passion" in 1932.[69] Furthermore, *Q.E.D.* is written in a mode far closer to realism than Stein's later work. Consequently, it might be viewed as an academic phase in the career's development and so not receive priority in efforts to publish Stein's work. It might also be more plainspoken about lesbianism, even to the uninitiated reader, than Stein's later, more experimental erotic texts. Whatever Stein's reasons, she buried the manuscript. Like many of her erotic texts, *Q.E.D.* was not published until after Stein's death (under the alternate title, *Things As They Are*). It was not released until 1950, although it did come out, so to speak, while Toklas was still alive, in an abridged form with a limited circulation of 516 copies. In 1971, after Toklas's death, Leon Katz issued the original *Q.E.D.* in full. Through this tortuous history, a secreted text came to light.

Q.E.D. was hardly exceptional among Stein's compositions for its lesbian content. Since the 1970s, much has been said and written, particularly by feminist literary critics, about Stein's encoding of lesbian/woman-identified sexual and bodily references within the full range of her work, particularly within her erotic poetry. Among these critics are Catharine Stimpson, Elizabeth Fifer, Lisa Ruddick, and Marianne DeKoven. Indeed, it has frequently been the case that discussion of codes in Stein's work has centered on sexuality in language. These critics have drawn attention, for example, to the pet terms Stein uses throughout her erotic work, including "Didn't Nelly and Lilly Love You," such as "caesar," "cow," and "fish." They have also assisted readers in identifying Stein's colloquial references to such sexual experiences as, for instance, orgasms as "coming." This work has proven most helpful in allowing readers to perform new, sex-positive readings of Stein, as well as to indicate fresh ways of approaching other aspects of the texts.

At the same time, the reader must bear in mind that Stein hardly buried these allusions in her texts. For example, in a single work of short fiction, "Miss Furr and Miss Skeene," Stein uses the word "gay" to describe these two central characters approximately 140 times.[70] While at the time of this publication the term was not as widely recognized a reference to homosexuality as it is today, its selection and frequency as a descriptor would certainly make any thoughtful reader reflect on the source of the women's rare "gaiety" together. As read by Judy Grahn, Stein's use of the word "gay" in "Miss Furr and Miss Skeene" does not suggest concealment of lesbian sexuality unless one believes that the frequency of the word's appearance in itself constitutes the act of hiding an object in plain view: "Instead of avoiding the subject out of fear of its taboo nature, she centered on it, taking advantage of its natural aboveground camouflage as a 'nice' word, which one would apply as a matter of course to 'nice young ladies' " (Grahn, 138–39). A case such as this one raises the issue of secrecy in inscription of lesbian sex in literature, for how secret is the language or message here? Lesbian sex is hardly concealed in these Stein compositions.

Even decades ago, critics reading Stein's erotic texts readily discerned their sexual nature. It is probable that the tendency to dismiss Stein's texts as nonsense had, at its base, much more to do with certain readers' distaste for the kind of sense these texts invited readers to make. In the words of Elizabeth Fifer, regarding such recoil on the part of homophobic readers, "Better that it should mean nothing than that it should mean *that* seems too often to have been the response. Critics preferred to focus on her 'nonsensical' grammatical usages rather than to encounter directly her sexually charged content."[71] At the same time, there is some suggestion in "Didn't Nelly and Lilly Love You" that Stein found these barriers to criticism functional. Making characteristic use of the male pronoun to refer to herself as writer, Stein writes, "Do you see why he wished to remain unintelligible. . . . For this reason and for this reason alone I have no opposition, I have no one in opposition. For . . . this reason I do not call subjects subjects" (N&L, 238). Other critics responded to Stein's sexual discourse with the verbal equivalent of a deep blush, by either remaining silent on the matter or expressing discomfort with the privacy of such textual encounters, as did Richard

Bridgman in comparing the experience of reading Stein's erotica to the work of monitoring the wiretap surveillance of a household. Stein, however, regarded all writing as a private act.

Of course, today's readers, more accustomed to private disclosures in literature, understand that revulsion or reticence need not be the only response to Stein's sexually rich texts. If we conduct readings of Stein as an intimate dialogue between reader and writer, then her erotic texts may suggest the most intimate such pairing. In this context, the performative act of reading approximates the act of lovemaking. Such is the clear suggestion of Rebecca Mark in her essay about "Lifting Belly": "There are many ways to make love to lifting belly. I will share one way—there are others, as many as we can live" (*LB*, iv). The embrace of the page by writer and reader becomes a tender exchange, a mutual act of loving attention at least as intimate as sex. Stein establishes this likeness in many of her works, as when, again invoking the male pronoun to describe herself, she establishes a parallel between "She with a sheet of linen and he with a sheet of paper," in "A Lyrical Opera Made By Two To Be Sung."[72] Writing takes on the character of an inky bliss, spilling over the pages and onto the reader.

The spiritual and sexual communion that *Q.E.D.*'s Adele sought in her quest and the gaiety of female friendship in "Miss Furr and Miss Skeene" in time become the subject and pageantry of many of Stein's other love writings. "Birth and Marriage," for example, appeared as a companion piece or sequel to the earlier "A Sonatina Followed By Another," forming a textual couple.[73] To someone unfamiliar with Stein's work, "Birth and Marriage" might seem an unlikely title for an erotic poem. Readers of Stein, however, will recognize in this title a (re)birth that comes with love's discovery and a marriage that refers not to legal matrimony but rather to lovers' sexual union, for "When all is said one is wedded to bed" (N&L, 223).

Redemptive sexual love in this poem begins with its first line: "Barring yesterday she was born today" (B&M, 175). That is to say, love represents rebirth. What preceded that love is of little consequence, for life begins with love's discovery. "Birth and Marriage" is nothing if not an announcement, something wholly conventional in Western society when a child is born (birth) or when a man and woman wed (marriage). It is less conventional, though, to announce love or lovemaking, particularly in the case of same-sex love. Stein's unabashed joy in that announcement poses the question, "Who is ashamed of an accompaniment" (B&M, 183). The effect of Stein's pronouncement parallels the liberating effect of newly found love, for with its assertions, acts of love begin to seem "As good as they are beautiful" (B&M, 185).

Internal evidence reveals the author's awareness that many people do not share her openness to sexual discourse. Over and over again, a critical voice in "Birth and Marriage" queries "Who says that." Stein responds to dissenting opinions by playing with conventions of the Western (Christian) marriage ceremony, such as "I do" (B&M, 197). By weaving together objections (for which the traditional wedding ceremony reserves a place) and the ceremony's central vow, "I do," the affirmation of love ("I do") becomes both a reaffirmation of the passions that brought the lovers to marriage and a defiant response to those who would silence passion's expression. In the lines above, Stein shows a progression of the critical voice, from "Who says that" to "Who says so" (197). Where initially the objection sought to identify a culprit, it later reaches a point where debate would be viable. By appropriating that critical voice in the poem, and incorporating it in her formulation of debate, Stein offers a new perspective on the dignity of love.

In so doing, Stein highlights a liminal situation, that in which lovers join. She employs the wedding ceremony with its procession to evoke that new beginning. Stein validates that lovers' union by declaring it "as considerable as birth" (and since birth may also be the result of such union among heterosexuals, she implicitly validates nonprocreative sex and same-sex pleasures, for both are "as considerable as birth"), with the result that lovers may give themselves to one another, to "Commence again seriously to delight." "Birth and Marriage" is a defense of sexual pleasure and sexual play ("ring around the rosy"). At the same time, it is also a testimony to the sacredness of love's redemptive powers. By invoking the traditions of a church wedding, Stein makes public and profound the union of lovers. She opens the doors of the church to unwed lovers, calling their bonds no less than wedded love, just as homosexual love is not less than heterosexual love. Both are divine, conjuring for Stein the image of a cross. Furthermore, for Stein, love is not lowered by its repeated sexual expression. "Birth and Marriage" represents Stein's announcement of the purity and spiritual power of all sexual love.

Similarly, when Stein composes "Didn't Nelly and Lilly Love You," she seems to be writing a valentine of sorts—both to Alice B. Toklas and to her readers. Like children's stories, made rich through the retelling, Stein's romance in "Didn't Nelly and Lilly Love You" is a welcome because familiar narrative pleasure: "And now for the story" (N&L, 229). Within her own relationship, the text does the work of recalling their acquaintance (made monumental in the recurrent references to "the meeting"), their courtship, their marriage, and their lives together (complete with the residue of jealousy over previous partners, as suggested by the piece's title). For readers aware of the Stein-Toklas relationship, the text operates as a tribute to their union. For readers unaware of that relationship, the text is still, as Rebecca Mark calls "Lifting Belly," a book to love. It brims with feeling, disclosure, confession, apology, and satisfaction, all suspended in a solution of personal and biographical references.

Even in an era during which biographical criticism of literature is unfashionable, then, it is difficult to avoid altogether in dealing with Stein's work. She gives the informed reader repeated reminders that the writer is present in the text, as where a line from "Didn't Nelly and Lilly Love You"—"She was born in California and he was born in Allegheny, Pennsylvania" (N&L, 224)—leaves little doubt that on some level the text's "she" is Toklas and "he" is Stein. Just as there is no real attempt to conceal the sexual nature of the text, and no attempt except some signature pronoun-switching to conceal the text's lesbian sexuality, Stein does not shield the fact that in her romances she inscribes her love for and relationship with Toklas. In her *Stein Reader* introduction to "As A Wife Has A Cow A Love Story," Ulla E. Dydo articulates this sense in which Toklas functions as a muse to Stein: "Alice Toklas makes writing possible in making living possible. Even in the first portrait *Ada*, the two figures, like lovers everywhere, never tire of telling and listening to love stories. Toklas is inside and outside all stories, inspiring, validating, listening, reciprocating. . . . In this fact, not in any theory, is the key to the life and work of Gertrude Stein. As making love concludes with the cow, so writing concludes with a book. Sexuality and writing become one. . . . All Stein's writings become love stories and all her work a single love story."[74] It seems true that, in public contexts, Tolkas preferred to downplay the sexual energy of Stein's writing. It seems equally true that she helped energize the texts. Companion, helpmate, caretaker, partner, inspiration, and ardent first audience, Toklas stirs Stein into making of artistic creation a kind of verbal lovemaking, particularly in terms of her erotic writing.

With "Didn't Nelly and Lilly Love You," Stein narrates a love relationship that is not without its opponents. As in "Birth and Marriage," a critical voice pierces the surface of the text, particularly in its open-

ing pages, asking "What did he say?" (N&L, 221). There are suggestions that the story's lovers must meet in secret: "And where do we
permit ourselves to declare our fond affection" (N&L, 224). The text
hints that the lovers are inhospitably observed, requiring them to
"alternate between hiding and precision" (N&L, 242). Even the text
seems to register some awareness of the spectator, as statements are
followed by denials, and the speaking voice warns that "I can erase
this" (N&L, 252).

In addition to the threat of surveillance by unsympathetic witnesses,
the central relationship in the text is itself marked by some discord.
The conflicts within this couple, however, are highly recognizable ones.
Each is concerned that the other is pleased. Each frets over the other's
devotion. At least one lover lingers over the knowledge of her beloved's
previous partners, as the title and its many echoes through the text suggest. These concerns at times turn the narrative from its primarily con-
versational tone to that of a dispute, as implied by statements of rebuttal. These contretemps are momentary, though, and attest to the
emotional closeness rather than the crisis of their relationship. They
form the dramatic counterpoint to the love letters passed between the
pair, as they anticipate "mingling their addresses" (N&L, 232). Funda-
mentally, the union appears a strong one, both emotionally and sexually,
and as the text proceeds, it is less impeded by thoughts of others,
whether witnesses or rivals. Pleasure and play abound for the pair. "If
fishes were wishes," writes Stein in images reminiscent of the fairy tale
of the fisherman and the magic fish, "the ocean would be all of our
desire" (N&L, 230).

As one reads Stein's erotic texts, such as "Didn't Nelly and Lilly Love
You," there is little doubt that Stein has turned Rose's mandala, "a rose
is a rose is a rose," into a Sapphic epicenter, "a bed of roses" (N&L,
236). With her writing, Stein found that "sentences came to make a
blessing" (N&L, 288). She appropriates, contests, and revises elements
of heterosexual romance—as lived and written—to write her way over
the threshold of a realm of women's sexual pleasure: "I gather from what
I saw at the door that you wanted me to come in before," and "she and
I never hesitated before that door" (N&L, 252, 232). It is a dwelling
place where frivolity is acceptable, a place where external labels fall
away, and identity becomes more internal and fluid. As Wayne Koestenbaum writes of this joyously destabilized signifier for homosexuality in
Stein's work, "What 'gay' means will not be decided; but you can follow
where 'gay' goes, how 'gay' moves, impatient and ambulatory, through

sentences—so that 'gay' begins to seem a drive or a propulsive force more than a stable attribute or personality characteristic."[75] Here, in Stein's erotic texts, women may engage each other at length without outside judgments or interferences: "I was not dreadfully embarrassed. I wasn't either. Nor was I at all troubled. Neither was I. Nor did I bother you. No you did not do that" (N&L, 243). Here, at least in language, Stein's women can express themselves freely, whether pitching woo, reminiscing about courtship, narrating and directing acts of lovemaking, discussing matters of relationship such as fidelity, offering thanks and reassurances, and rejoicing in relationship and its renewal. Stein writes her characters into a place of woman-identified reverie.

Stein's texts create ample opportunities for reflection of this kind, including thoughts about the implication of Stein's use of the formulas of the popular romance. Playing teasingly with, and ultimately setting aside, the devices of homosexual masking or passing, Stein delivers pages unmistakably steeped in lesbian sexuality. This forthright expression of homosexuality, as Rebecca Mark has observed, is "not lesbian sex, over there in the closet, hidden in bed, away from the public eye. Lifting belly is lesbian sex in the world, participating, relating and transforming everything it encounters" (*LB*, xix). Just as she found ways to enliven the writing of children's stories through backtalk, Stein found through Sapphic modernism a means to revive the romance as a literary form. Like her other erotic writings, "Didn't Nelly and Lily Love You" is a recovered story of recognizable feeling, retold in the familiar terms of the romance, and so saved from silence and protected from treatment as anomaly. Bearing much in common with heterosexual love stories, the text, as Stein herself writes, "is the history of wishes guessed expressed and gratified" (N&L, 230). In recording that history through the familiar form of the romance, Stein claims it on behalf of the "love that dare not speak its name." Stein is not simply encoding, then, but recoding the conventions of popular literary genres, such as the romance. She is not fashioning a cipher so much as refashioning the ciphers already in cultural and linguistic place. Through the framing of her woman-loving poems and stories, Stein discovers that "Romance is delicious" (*GHA*, 165).

Like her use of the word "gay," Stein's use of the adjective "queer" in her works seems a deliberate affirmation in the face of social stigma. In the opening pages of Stein's generational saga of the Hersland family, *The Making of Americans*, Stein suggests that the country is seriously wanting in genuine expressions of cultural difference: "Now singularity that is neither crazy, faddish, or a fashion, or low class with distinction, such a singularity, I say, we have not made enough of yet so that any other one can really know it, it is as yet an unknown product with us. It takes time to make queer people, and to have others who can know it, time and a certainty of place and means" (*TMOA*, 21). As Wayne Koestenbaum has aptly noted, "The best single adjective to describe Stein's sensibility and style is 'queer,' not simply because of the word's association with sex-and-gender ambiguity, but because of the word's evocation of what is simultaneously *uncanny* and *pleasure-giving* in a phenomenon's or a person's refusal to match a predetermined grid. . . . A word or a category is queered when it slips away from what it has been" (Koestenbaum, 305). Stein's efforts toward "vital singularity" are written across her career (*TMOA*, 21). They do not appear in code, but neither do they speak plainly. Her work is "queer," and so is she, insofar as her life and her writing respect few preset boundaries, whether of gender or genre.

In this way, it is possible to read such seemingly disparate Stein texts as *The World Is Round*, "Did Nelly and Lilly Love You?" and *Blood on the Dining-Room Floor* as documents of desire: the detective story (the desire to uncover a secret), the children's story (the desire to know what comes next), and the love story (the desire to know others and to be known). Stein plays with these familiar desires, as well as the literary formulas of their expression, both gratifying and thwarting the reader's expectations.

It might be fair to say, then, that Gertrude Stein's short fiction operates by turns as a window, a mirror, and an open closet door. Her writings provide a window to the hidden private world and its clues, as when she writes using the quintessential genre of surveillance, the detective story. Stein's texts also hold up a mirror to the "looking glass society," as when she calls attention to the gendered limits of magic in conventional children's fiction, as well as the consequences that await characters who transgress these limits. With her erotic fiction, Stein throws open the door of closeted sexuality to claim for herself the love story as narrative form.

In a world of fiction, where the imperative is pointedly to show and not tell, Stein dedicates herself instead to telling. In the detective story, the sleuth has the role of telling others the story of the crime. In the children's story, a narrator reveals the events and outcomes of a story's familiar premise. In the love story, partners tell their feelings and profess their devotions. Through these acts of telling, Stein's short fiction functions as a sexual coming-out narrative, complete with its phases of secrecy, denial, surveillance, exploration, disclosure, assertion, and acceptance. This theme of an unmasked sexuality, whether confessional or celebratory in tone, permeates Stein's work. As a result, Stein's writings frequently echo the coming-out narrative, with its performance and claiming of a once-concealed identity. In Stein's words, "it takes time to make queer people."

The Question of Camp

Camp is to gay what soul is to black.

—Dennis Altman

Camp is the answer to the problem: how to be a dandy in the age of mass culture.

—Susan Sontag

Camp is a lie that tells the truth.

—Philip Core

Generous readers of Stein have often found humor in her writing and its appropriations of popular narrative forms. It should in no way diminish the sense of her literary importance to acknowledge that she frequently accomplished her work through the definitive devices of performative humor: asides, raucous one-liners, parody, wordplay, and free associa-tion. Others who have sought to read Stein's work, even some sympa-thetic readers, have either failed to appreciate its humor or found them-selves unsure how to react. Is it permissible to laugh at a legacy? Would it be appropriate to respond to modernist experimentalism with laugh-ter? Does the author intend that her readers laugh? Still, much of Stein's writing may be engaged as in large measure an overture to the reader's sense of irony, as a movement to "place the laughing where the smile is" (LGB, 97). Once the reader allows herself to receive the humor of Stein's prose, there is a nearly conspiratorial pleasure in gos-siping and laughing along with Stein. In much the same way that pop icon Andy Warhol was known to spectate and pronounce everything he saw "great," Stein's humor, as Judy Grahn notes, "is that of the essential geni, the 'idiot' or king's fool who sees the emperor naked and finds this nakedness wonderfully interesting, or who finds something else entirely about the situation wonderfully interesting" (Grahn, 19). The reader prepared to find comedy in Stein's writing will read her differently, will attend to the many ways in which her texts function as high-spirited conversations (both among the voices within the text and between writer and reader). Although one's first impulse might be to stifle or disallow laughter, perhaps out of concern that the response not seem dismissive, something precious is lost if a reader becomes too sober in the process. Many key texts of modernism have had their signatures and sources in humor; after all, both Virginia Woolf's *Orlando* and Gertrude Stein's *Autobiography of Alice B. Toklas* began as jokes.

How, then, might one engage or understand the humor of Stein's compositions? Over the years, readers have puzzled over the prose and the persona, the words and the ways of a writer who felt little obligation to their literary or social expectations. There is a rich irony, for instance, in the most common objection made to Stein's prose style: claims of its endless repetition. Indeed, it was because Stein was so resolute in avoiding imitation of previous writing that her work reads so distinctively, relatively free of allusions to or reinscriptions of earlier texts. While it is easy to see how Stein influenced those writers who came after her, it is much more difficult to name her origins, largely because her work sets about building a vocabulary of internal (rather than intertextual) referents, whose recurrence within and across Stein texts most likely made it seem repetitive to readers seeking the familiar sense of affirmation that comes only from reading what they have read before— re-reading. By her straying from, rather than revering, the "original" of the canon, Stein "reveals the original to be nothing other than a parody of the *idea* of the natural and the original."[76] Like Shakespeare's Puck wandering into the pages of "The Emperor's New Clothes," Stein makes the point that one need not disrobe the literary forebears to see their nakedness. One needs only to look.

Stein then not only proclaims that the twentieth century's "only real literary thinking" has been done by a woman, she goes so far as to "come out" to her readers as that very woman. She is the self-declared literary genius. By these lights, her work, especially its brazen verbal pose, was unruly and deviant. It seemed to many observers to require firm discipline: at the least, her work needed an edit for punctuation and capitalization; at most, it needed to be discredited. For her willingness to set aside literary categories, grammatical pieties, and generic niceties, Stein was dismissed, decried, or labeled as Other. As a result, Stein has been alternately cast as a diseased mind, a bourgeois aesthete, a fraud, a counterfeit, a hoax, a freak, unnatural, mannered, effete, esoteric, an impersonator, and an imposter. The accusations, taken together, constitute a familiar list of epithets not for literary figures but for the gay and lesbian subculture—its style, sensibility, and ways of living in the world.

While many of these criticisms of Stein's work are likely the product of homophobia and could now be dismissed as such, there remains the issue of how to read Stein's works and what we have come to recognize as, in the finest and comedic sense, their textual homophilia.

Shifts in the ways readers have received the erotic contents of Stein's work represent a case in point. Since the 1970s, feminist critics have begun to attend to the sexual register of Stein's writing in those texts identified as homoerotic. Their efforts have recuperated a Stein almost lost to us through the denouncements and negations of earlier detractors. Such revisionist critics have done much to recall to us the vitality and urgency in reclaiming Stein's woman-loving texts from "Lifting Belly" to "Pink Melon Joy." What we have yet to do, however, in reading Stein is to lavish attention on the further implications of approaching Stein through the lens of gay/lesbian/bisexual/transgender studies and queer theory. That is, how do we engage Stein as a woman-identified writer, including the ways that identity becomes complicated by her writing pose (complete with her use of male pronouns)? How do we perform queer readings of Stein, including readings that look at the less celebratory voices of her lesbianism? How do Stein readers construct a texuality/sexuality whose influences are written not only in passages about sex acts but those about the acts of living as an outsider and writing as a woman-loving woman? What are we to make of Stein's mingling of concealment and disclosure, candor and camouflage, when it comes to her place in gay and lesbian literature and culture? How, too, do we reckon her relationship to paradox, marginality, and humor?

One tempting approach is to think about Stein in terms of literary camp, a stylized sensibility historically associated with homosexual cultural statement. The word *camp* has its beginnings in the French verb *se camper*, first used to describe the pronounced postures of melodrama. By the 1920s, the word became a slang term for homosexual. It subsequently became associated with a very particular style of cultural counterstatement, one preoccupied with incongruity and marginality. According to Sue-Ellen Case, "Camp both articulates the lives of homosexuals through the obtuse tone of irony and inscribes their oppression with the same device. Likewise, it eradicates the ruling powers of heterosexist realist modes."[77] Could it be that Stein's "murder" of the nineteenth-century's worn-out, literary language was also an erasure of its oppressive uses of heterosexist realism? Viewed through the context of camp—whether the dandyism of Oscar Wilde, the cross-dressing of women on the left bank, or the outrageous stage whisper of modernist masquerade—Stein's work, and its history of reception, may become easier to see and narrate as comedic counterstatement.

The phenomenon of camp has been defined variously. Nonetheless, there are some matters about which there is some measure of consensus:

> First, everyone agrees that camp is a style (whether of objects or of the way objects are perceived is debated) that favors "exaggeration," "artifice," and "extremity." Second, camp exists in tension with popular culture, commercial culture, or consumerist culture. Third, the person who can recognize camp, who sees things as campy, or who can camp is a person outside the cultural mainstream. Fourth, camp is affiliated with homosexual culture, or at least with a self-conscious eroticism that throws into question the naturalization of desire.[78]

Camp has been characterized as the voice that speaks in italics, that places all words in quotation marks, that winks continuously at the utterance in progress. Camp can also be, as some have noted "subversive—a means of illustrating those cultural ambiguities and contradictions that oppress us all, gay and straight, and, in particular, women."[79] Adjectives used to characterize camp include esoteric, stylized, aesthetic, artificial, fantastic, glamorous, extravagant, theatrical, affected, exaggerated, textured, and passionate. Is it mere coincidence that camp is extreme and outlandish in many of the precise ways—whether moral or expressive—readers have experienced Stein's texts to be?

Readers and critics have sought, over the past few decades, to articulate and deepen their sense of the pleasure in/of Stein's unruly texts, a kind of fun too long forbidden. Increasingly, readers have permitted themselves to play with, and to sense the play within, Stein's compositions. This new receptiveness to textual whimsy and playfulness has been very productive of understanding. In order to view this shift in the context of camp, it is only a small stretch from the spirit of wordplay to the ambience of stage-, role-, and gender-play. Throughout her oeuvre, Stein makes of literary custom a costume, to be donned and shed at (her) will, an occasion for irreverence and wry glance. In Stein's work, past literature's reliance upon literary convention begins to resemble a compulsion, to be tempered with absurdity and remediated with transgressive joy. Protocols of genre, narratology, dialogue, and characterization fall away as Stein refuses to take any of it too seriously. Instead, Stein struts across the page, flaunting her difference and wearing the mantle of the poets as if it were an ostrich boa. As writer Esther Newton points out, "Incongruity is the subject matter of camp, theatricality its style, and humor its strategy."[80] Could it be that the gleeful resistence of and in Stein's texts operates through the medium of literary camp?

If one looks at the key camp figures of her day, as Philip Core has done in his book, *Camp: The Lie That Tells the Truth,* it becomes clear that Gertrude Stein knew, knew of, had dealings with, and wrote about many of the greats: Guillaume Apollinaire, Sir Frederick Ashton, Djuna Barnes, Sir Cecil Beaton, Nathalie Clifford Barney, Jean Cocteau, Colette, Edith Sitwell, Ronald Firbank, and Carl Van Vechten.[81] Some, such as Van Vechten, she knew well. In later years, he would serve as her literary executor. For that matter, Stein herself appears in Core's guidebook to camp, where she is remembered for her "solitude, oracular attitude and masculine intelligence" (Core, 174). In addition to her circle of acquaintance, another formative influence on the camp-informed Stein persona was her residence in Paris. In the years during which Stein came into her own as an adult and as a woman, years spent in Paris, the city was becoming not simply a haven for expatriate writers and artists but also something of an international capital for free-thinking and woman-loving women.

Given her lesbianism, Stein might well have lived as an expatriate of sorts at home in the States. Instead, she built a life in France, where she and Alice B. Toklas were relatively free to live and associate as they saw fit. Sandra Gilbert and Susan Gubar capture this ambience in their description of Paris in the 1920s: "Indeed, certain neighborhoods in Paris may have seemed—at least to sophisticated visitors—like the eroticized quarters of a city of ladies in which lesbian artists could evolve exclusive coteries based on their defiance of conventional codes of behavior and their present of an artistry linked to their love affairs" (Gilbert and Gubar, 219). Stein found in Paris a subcultural mecca, where she and Toklas could pursue their lives and their work—the collaboration on her literary ventures—together, with minimal outside impediments. They positioned themselves, through location and material ease, to comment on the society that otherwise would have them occupy the margin. This double consciousness of the expatriate and lesbian finds expression through camp.

Most camp experiences are lived and/or performed. Some, however, may take the form of performative literary experiences. Wayne Dynes, in his *Encyclopedia of Homosexuality,* suggests that when camp "is verbal, it is expressed less through the discursive means of direct statement than through implication, innuendo, and intonation. As an art of indirection and suggestion, it was suited to the purposes of a group that found it imprudent to confront culturally approved values directly, but preferred to undermine them through send-ups and sly mockery."[82] Writings from Walt Whitman's "Song of Myself" to Allen Ginsberg's "A Supermarket in California," Oscar Wilde's *Portrait of Dorian Gray* to Marcel Proust's *A la recherche du temps perdu,* have given us landmarks of literary camp. According to Karl Keller,

> In literature, camp appears in the form of the epiphanal tease, the theatricalization of a narrator, character, or point of view, the use of extreme mannerisms as personality gestures, the invention of awkward intensities in syntax or metaphor, the mock-play with inflated conventions of narration and characterization, extravagance of style as a disguise for the writer, the tone of voice that is "too much" and therefore entertaining in its flamboyant playfulness.[83]

Once again, the description of camp seems to echo crucial features, whether beloved or derided, observed by Stein's readers over the years. With her pen, Stein sets in ink the four basic features of the expressive domain of camp: "irony, aestheticism, theatricality, and humor" (Babuscio, 20). Stein's irreverence for literary standards, from chapter structure to genre boundary, certainly strikes a pose of refusal toward received culture and its strictures.

Perhaps the greatest impediment to reading Stein through camp has been the same one that has blocked encounter with gay literature more generally: denial. As David Bergman writes in "Strategic Camp: The Art of Gay Rhetoric,"

> To those looking in on camp, its style seems flat and extreme; consequently, the heterosexual readers' response to overtly gay literature is always problematical, especially when the literature is particularly campy. Usually the problem has been masked by denial of the homosexual or campy component (as in the case of Whitman), hostility, or avoidance.... Rarely have straight critics—especially straight male critics—acknowledged that their difficulties with a work are related to issues of gender. At a conference I heard Charles Molesworth, Charles Altieri, and Cary Nelson complain that they could not locate the tone of several passages in James Merrill's poetry. At first, none of these ostensibly heterosexual readers was willing to admit his inability to recognize camp and shifted the blame for the "indeterminacy" of tone onto Merrill.[84]

For years the dominant voices in literary criticism have overlooked, or actively sought to look past, the nuanced and gendered voices of gay literature, instead pronouncing that literature uninteresting, ambiguous, or indeterminate. That had, until recently, certainly been the case for Stein. As early as 1914, an anonymous reviewer for the *Atlantic Monthly* deemed Stein's work beyond understanding, calling it "a sedative of flat prose from the paper."[85] Just as the attempts to engage Merrill's poetry result in accusations of flat and indeterminate writing, readers of Stein have often assumed that textual defects explain their frustrated attempts at constructing meanings. Her writings, these readers insist, have somehow failed them.

By virtue of the very ways in which camp functions in a text, though, as a kind of double-talk (addressing itself on one level to members of a subculture, on another to a general readership), writers such as Stein have risked refusal in order to bring into speech an argot of self-recognition, connection, and survival. Rather than repressing or encoding these impulses, the writers in question place the camp message in plain sight, for the like-minded spectator to find and others to fail to notice. In so doing, literary camp "is the 'secret' that privileges the homosexual reader. What renders it effective is, precisely, the distance heterosexuals are determined to keep between themselves and the very idea of homosexuality. It is a distance leaving ample space for irony."[86] Just as Toni Morrison speaks of her practice of leaving spaces for the reader to speak in and through her texts, writers of literary camp—Stein included—create room for gay and lesbian readers to claim and inhabit literary texts in ways all their own. Heterosexuals can and do read these texts in engaged ways; they just are less likely to discern some of the humor and subtext that form the signatures of literary camp. Their readings may be satisfying, if selective, but will prove distinct from those produced by the spectator prepared for the provocative play and subversive inscription of camp.

If camp takes its origins from audacious pose, then Gertrude Stein certainly presented herself in such terms. She toyed with her public identity in much the same way she toyed with her appearance. As critics such as Susan Gubar and Marjorie Garber observe, Stein was one of many female modernists who engaged in cross-dressing as a transgressive act.[87] Stein and her Sapphic contemporaries, through their appropriations of male attire, pose, and prose, not only performed a critique of the gender expectations of a patriarchal society but also of the gendered idioms of modernism. Gubar finds that "the women who helped form what we too often consider the exclusively male movement of modernism exploited transvestism only initially to in-vest the traditional form of patriarchy with authority, for ultimately such artists divest conventional forms of legitimacy and, finally, as the etymology of the word transvestite implies, they do this to make the travesty of sexual signs" (Gubar, 502). By claiming for themselves the trappings of male and female identity markers alike, women writers such as Stein helped to dislodge the visual signs of reified gender identity in literature and life. In so doing, they sought to blur the ink of appearance as the "signature to a [fixed, stable, unitary] cultural identity."[88]

By her own and others' accounts, there were many Steins: (1) the *maternal saint* immortalized in Jo Davidson's sculpture of her; (2) the *image of domesticity*, as she, bedecked with flowered hat, joins Toklas to feed the Venice pigeons; (3) the poetic *priestess* holding court at 27 Rue de Fleurus, attired in a floor-length velvet robe, her hair pinned in a bun; (4) the *goddess*, as seen in the Lipchitz portrait head; (5) the *twin*, posing for a photograph in her salon, seated beneath Picasso's cubist portrait of her; (6) the cropped-hair *monk*, seen in publicity photographs (with and without Toklas) for her American tour; (7) the living *deity*, as Gubar notes, in Cecil Beaton's photographs of her in flowing fabrics at Bilignin; (8) the *ancient*, complete with attire worthy of a Roman senator; (9) the *Grecian sibyl* in Picabia's 1933 portrait of her or in classical drapery in Francis Rose's (unpainted) study of Stein; (10) the *sturdy soldier*, donning thick coats, full-length skirts, and long-sleeved blouses to greet soldiers abroad; (11) the *Buddha* seated on an outdoor tabletop in Fiesole; (12) the *madcap humpty-dumpty* seated on the wall to sing her favorite, "Trail of the Lonesome Pine"; (13) the *serene prophet*, in a kimono, hands folded, as drawn by Djuna Barnes; (14) the *peasant in steerage*, as Ernest Hemingway saw her; (15) the *Aztec figure in obsidian* as described by friend Harold Acton; (16 and 17) the *literary royal* on her throne and the *mystic* pressing pen to a glowing page, as photographed by Alvin Langdon Coburn; (18) the long-cloaked *visionary* complete with beads in Felix Valloton's 1907 portrait; (19 and 20) the *leopard-hatted boheme* and the *dictator on art*, as seen by photographer Man Ray; (21) the *emblem of movement* both literal and literary, in Imogen Cunningham's multiple exposure of Stein, registering the writer in permanent movement; (22) the *benevolent viking* noted by *The Nation* on her lecture tour; (23) the *merry man* that newspapers said looked like something out of Robin Hood's forest; (24) the *Napoleonic figure* whose millinery acquaintance Bravig Imbs described as severe and excessively mannish;

(25) the *roman general,* an image that had some of her acquaintances calling her Caesar; (26) the *gypsy queen* as seen by Nathalie Clifford Barney;, (27) the *handsome Jewish patriarch,* as seen by Katherine Anne Porter; (28) the *Easter Island idol* observed by Edith Sitwell; (29) the *weather-beaten Cape Cod fisherman* reporters described upon her arrival in the States; and (30 and 31) the *Indian chief* in Carl Van Vechten's photographs, where she appears with shoulder wrapped in fabric to resemble white representations of Native Americans, or alternately imagined by Van Vechten as the *Yankee Doodle dandy* posed before the American flag.

Stein relished the image-making possibilities, as when she used the windfall from the success of *The Autobiography of Alice B. Toklas* to purchase a new wardrobe. Her look—and with it, people's ways of seeing her—shifted frequently, as the often-repeated anecdote from Picasso attests. When viewers of his portrait of Stein told the painter that it did not resemble the writer, Picasso assured them that it soon would. The core elements of self-presentation remained somewhat routine—a fondness for long skirts, sandals, and ornate waistcoats—but the nuances of result and perceptions of it were ever shifting. William Gass may have summed up the effect tellingly when, in his introduction to the *Geographical History of America*—the text Thornton Wilder called "a work of gaiety"—Gass characterized Stein as "queerly companioned and oddly dressed" (*GHA*, 50, 22).

In this way, Stein manufactured a public persona, a queer pose suiting her wish to create a very particular image. She functioned as a dandy, more Oscar Wilde than Yankee Doodle. A reference within her early novella, *Fernhurst,* establishes that Stein was aware of Wilde. How well she knew his work or biography is not known. Nonetheless, camp, a phenomenon closely associated with Wilde, offered another marker of Stein's position as a social and literary outsider. Far from a mere digression or conceit, camp performed a valuable kind of work for Stein as writer. Stein found in camp simultaneously a vehicle to challenge literary standards of value and taste, a means to work critically with the formulas of popular literature, a tempering effect to keep modernism from taking itself too seriously, and an opportunity to rewrite and inhabit fictional worlds that never had her or her lover in mind.

As a lesbian, Stein brought her own perspective to both high and low literary forms, helping modernism cross the great divide through the camp sensibility. Stein appropriates these texts and forms to make them her own. Mindful of the role mass culture was beginning to play in solidifying and connecting members of subcultures, Stein did not dismiss any popular form as void or lowbrow. Neither did she love these forms uncritically; witness her cutting remarks about print journalism in *Lectures in America*.[89] Through the refiguring of mass-cultural forms, though, Stein was able to enjoy their immediacy and gratifying shapes. By means of camp, Stein invoked genres of popular literature to reveal and comment on the ironies of her life and career. In one such irony, Stein found the means at once to overstate and celebrate her persona for, as Susan Sontag writes, camp, "even when it reveals self-parody, reeks of self-love."[90] By refusing to recede from the reading experience, Stein calls continuous attention to her presence as the writer of her texts.

Although camp, as subcultural affirmation, does not confine itself to a single culture or historical moment, there appear to be certain social conditions that make camp both more necessary and more possible to sustain. That is to say, camp is mostly a modern phenomenon. As spectacle, it implies an audience, a public expression. It lampoons bastions of bourgeois complacency and respectability: business, family, marriage, and convention. At the same time, to perform this work in public ways, camp must bound its subversions to some degree "for it depends for its survival on the patronage of high society, the entertainment world, advertising, and the media" (Dynes, 189). According to Dynes, for all these reasons, camp exists in a deeply ambivalent interdependence with mass culture. Camp's roots in mass culture's ambience of "doubt, alienation, relativism, and pluralism" (Dynes, 190) may also help account for Dynes's claim that the Third World has no counterpart to Western camp.

By dispensing with pretension and placing at the center of its discourse texts and experiences "devalued or repressed, thus providing a strategy for rewriting and questioning the meanings and values of mainstream representations," camp may indeed prove to be "gay culture's crucial contribution to modernism."[91] As Daniel Harris has argued, mass media had already helped "unite and nationalize the [gay] subculture."[92] Mass culture had, through such devices as underground magazines and pulp fiction, enhanced the means for subcultural reading, connectedness, and identity exploration. Camp, however, made it possible to articulate subcultural experience *and* point out the potential for subcultural readings of, and analysis of subcultural inflections to be found within, dominant cultural production. Camp could appropriate mainstream representations in popular culture to tell different stories, to "queer" readings of discourses that position themselves as resolutely heterosexual. In this sense, it becomes clear that it is not an object that is camp, but the form and manner of its scrutiny, display, or appropriation. It is not the cultural product—a Judy Garland concert, a Tallulah Bankhead motion-picture character, a Marlene Dietrich delivery of a song—but its process of delectation that renders it camp. It is a specifically mediated experience rather than a self-contained text.

Therefore, by cultivating irreverence for high literature and appropriating popular cultural literary forms (such as detective, children's, and erotic fiction), Stein could do with the writing of literature what she did with the performance of gender; she mixed genres and refused the heterosexual generic. In the process, she did not merely create new genres. Instead, she moved beyond categories to "tell it" in ways that rethought but did not reiterate existing literary forms, high or low. A camp reading of Stein's writing, and of readers' reactions to Stein's work, helps complicate our sense of Stein's paradise of paradox, where irony not orthodoxy rules.

When Gass described Gertrude Stein as "queerly companioned and oddly dressed," he might just as well have been describing Stein's short fiction. In Stein's stories, she combines language experiments of modernism with the emergent narrative forms of mass culture. Cubism and children's literature, portraits and pulp fiction, manifestoes and moon-and-june romances converge. Therefore, the language of Stein's short fiction is indeed "oddly dressed," as she makes companions of highbrow and lowbrow narrative modes in order to tell unconventional stories of her own. Following neither precedent nor fashion, Stein turned out texts in spectacularly different garb, at once recognizable and shocking.

What Becomes a Legend:
Reading the Popular through
Gertrude Stein

It was always Stein's contention that her writing would find real acceptance only with the passing decades. She insisted that once the society caught up with what she was doing in her work, she would be recognized and glorified as a literary lion, however belatedly. While for reasons both biographical and bibliographical Stein still does not stand in the high-modernist canon, her place in literary and women's history nonetheless now seems assured. Her name even appears in E. D. Hirsch's controversial *Cultural Literacy: What Every American Needs to Know* (1987) and *Dictionary of Cultural Literacy* (1988). Today's bookstore patrons often can find several of Stein's works available in paperback, and at Barnes and Noble bookstores can take home those purchases in a shopping bag emblazoned with Stein's serene likeness. She has become a literary and pop icon.

Given Stein's customary—and campy—bluster in writing about her own impact on American literature, it is difficult to say that she would be surprised by the resurgence in critical and popular interest in her work. In literature, there is little question that Stein's writing shapes the work of contemporaries and later figures, including Kathy Acker, Sherwood Anderson, Rae Armantrout, Djuna Barnes, Jane Bowles, Christine Brooke-Rose, Barbara Buiest, Maxine Chernoff, Laura Chester, Tina Darrach, Lydia Davis, H.D., Eva Figes, Carla Harryman, Marianne Hauser, Ernest Hemingway, Bernadette Mayer, Ursule Molinaro, Anaïs Nin, Rochelle Owens, Ann Quin, Jean Rhys, Judith Johnson Sherwin, Edith Sitwell, Virgil Thomson, Anne Waldman, Diane Ward, William Carlos Williams, and Marguerite Young.

Furthermore, she had both affection for and an impact on painting. Beyond Charles Demuth's poster *Love, Love, Love,* Francis Rose's watercolor study *Homage to Gertrude Stein,* Juan Gris's *Roses for Gertrude Stein,* and Picasso's *Homage to Gertrude* or *Still Life with Calling Card,* which all bear her mark, there are also more recent examples such as Willem

DeKoonig's Woman paintings, which the artist acknowledges were consciously created under Stein's influence.

Along with feminist and other scholars who have, in the past two decades, reclaimed Stein's work as power and precedent, people outside the academy have of late shown a good deal of their own interest in Stein as a figure. With this book's emphasis on Stein's relationship to mass culture and its narrative forms, it seems fitting to observe that beyond her impact on other experimental writers—considerable though that impact remains—Stein also has inspired contemporary workers in many mass media. A recounting of some examples may begin to dramatize how Stein continues to shape our popular as well as academic culture. The objective, then, is not to perform a close reading of each Stein-influenced text identified here but rather to point out how plentiful and sundry are these appropriations of Stein's cultural capital, whatever one takes that currency now to be. In painting, literature, tourism, comic strips, satire, detective fiction, poetry, opera, parody, children's literature, theater, ballet, puppet shows, the Internet, motion pictures, popular song, and still other formats, cultural representations of Stein, her persona, and her work remind us that she does not simply belong to the first half of the twentieth century. Nor is she on the mind of painters and creative writers alone. In an exceedingly wide range of cultural productions, readers of Stein find themselves reminded of a common refrain in Stein's texts, "When this you see, remember me." Both an image of Eucharist and eulogy, this phrase evokes Stein's yearning to be kept in mind, both during and beyond readings of her texts. She did not mean to recede into literary or cultural obscurity.

She has not been forgotten. Of course, the broadest spectrum of allusions to Stein occurs in print texts. In addition, then, to publications of Stein's work and Stein biography and criticism, a number of recent books invoke or seek to shape Stein's legacy for a popular audience. Those intrigued by Stein's life can draw from Mary Ellen Haight's 1988 volume, *Walks in Gertrude Stein's Paris*.[93] Aided by this book, readers can take tours of places frequented by Stein and Toklas during their time in France. Tom Hachtman's now out-of-print volume, *Fun City*, brings together Gertrude Stein and Alice B. Toklas with the comic strip as popular form.[94] Stein's caricature has also graced the pages of the *National Lampoon*, where she appears as a baseball tyrant, Gertrude Steinbrenner. It seems somehow fitting that long-time Stein and Toklas associate Samuel Steward commemorated their relationship to detective fiction—and to each other—in a trilogy of detective novels: *Murder is Murder is Murder* (1985), *The Caravaggio Shawl: A Gertrude Stein-Alice B. Toklas Mystery* (1989), and a third volume yet to appear.[95] Karren L. Alenier's *Bumper Cars: Gertrude Said She Took Him for a Ride* presents poetry inspired by the life and writings of Gertrude Stein, along with a libretto offered in the same spirit: "Gertrude Stein Invents a Jump Early On."[96]

Barbie Unbound, a 1997 collection of photographs by Geoff Hansen and essays by Sarah Strohmeyer critiquing the phenomenon generated by Mattel's Barbie doll, finds Stein and Toklas with another cameo appearance.[97] The book's premise is that an animate Barbie is accidentally packed with the textbooks from a mother's feminist literature class— Deirdre English, Barbara Ehrenreich, and Laura Mulvey. *Barbie Unbound* is the outcome of that chance meeting. Among images of Barbie as Joan of Arc, Anita Hill, and Marie Curie, the book features Gertrude Stein and Alice Toklas as something of a divine couple, as well as a welcome antidote to the narrowly prescriptive fantasy life afforded Mattel's Barbie. Here the two are invoked as "Barbie Stein and Midge B. Toklas," a quirky send-up, simultaneously recasting both their roles and those of the fashion- and merchandise-conscious dolls, Barbie and Midge. *Barbie Unbound* finds Stein and Toklas depicted as transgressive Barbies ("Barbie Stein and Midge B. Toklas and their Paris [Hair] Salon"), along with Picasso and Hemingway as reluctant Kens, clients in the hair salon.

In a less comic vein, Bertha Harris's *Gertrude Stein* (Lives of Notable Gay Men and Lesbians) and Ann LaFarge's *Gertrude Stein* (American Women of Achievement) bring to young adult readers the biography of Gertrude Stein. At the head of Joan Nestle's piece on lesbian literature in Robert Giard's *Particular Voices: Portraits of Gay and Lesbian Writers* (1997), a cardboard likeness of Stein poses in a photo entitled, "The Ghost of Gertrude Stein visits the Lesbian Herstory Archives." In 1997 Stein, along with Marcel Duchamp, also provided the premise for a Guggenheim Museum exhibition and catalogue, *Rrose is a Rrose is a Rrose: Gender Performance in Photography.*[98]

Neither does Stein's import for the theater go unnoticed. A wide variety of her compositions have been staged, including *Brewsie and Willie; Doctor Faustus Lights the Lights; Four Saints in Three Acts; Gertrude Stein First Reader; I am I Because My Little Dog Knows Me; In Circles; In a Garden; Ladies' Voices; Listen to Me; Look and Long; A Lyrical Opera Made By Two; A Manior; The Mother of Us All; Photograph; Play I (–III); A Wedding Bouquet; What Happened; When This You See, Remember Me;* and *Yes Is For a Very Young Man.* Her plays have assumed the forms of opera, ballet, marionette shows, and hypertexts. She has influenced both playwrights and perfor-

mance/mixed-media artists, including David Antin, John Cage, Allan
Kaprow, Dick Higgins, Richard Foreman, Jerome Rothenberg, Jackson
MacLow, Mac Wellman, David Greenspan, and Suzan-Lori Parks. In
addition to stagings of Stein's texts, numerous contemporary plays pay
homage to Stein as playwright and personality: Marty Martin's *Gertrude
Stein, Gertrude Stein, Gertrude Stein: A One Character Play;* La Mama's
Gertrude; William Michael Collins's *I Am I* and *Look at Me Now and Here I
Am: The One Man Show of Gertrude Stein;* Win Wells's *Gertrude Stein and a
Companion;* Thomas Leabhart's *A Simple Thing;* and Lila Pashalinski and
Linda Chapman's *Gertrude and Alice: A Likeness to Loving* among them.

Australian playwright Sandra Shotlander's *Framework* introduces its
central characters in a museum, before a portrait of Gertrude Stein and
a painting by Georgia O'Keeffe. In this way, Stein and O'Keeffe become
a presence, a frame, for the unfolding relationship between two women.

> Iris: She told me I'd see Picasso's Stein here. Stein's a hero of
> mine.
> Lee: Mine, too.
> Iris: Quite an eccentric.
> Lee: Monumental. Mind you, she had the money to be what-
> ever she wanted.
> Iris: Do you think it takes money?
> Lee: Helps—or courage or something.
> Iris: [*Looking at the portrait*] She's tight lipped. She's not giving
> anything away.
> Lee: I wish she would speak. I've been haunting this corner
> lately. It has a power. Can you feel it?[99]

The play's two central characters, Lee and Iris, speak to their "hero"
(shero?), sensing, though not yet articulating, their need for her influence. She stands for something important, and the characters step
through the frame of Picasso's portrait of Stein to a sitting room where
their relationship to one another, and to Stein, emerges.

In the same spirit as these dramatic tributes, motion pictures have
also announced their debt to Stein. Allusions in mainstream films
appear in *Bye Bye Birdie, Top Hat,* and *The Man on the Flying Trapeze.* A
spate of recent arthouse films focus on modernist writers during the
1920s and 1930s, such as Philip Kaufman's *Henry and June* (1990) Brian
Gilbert's *Tom and Viv* (1994), Alan Rudolph's *Mrs. Parker and the Vicious
Circle* (1994), and Sally Potter's *Orlando* (1993). Additionally, Stein's

words are quoted in a wide range of contemporary women's films, including Ulrike Ottinger's 1979 *Bildnis einer Trinkerin* (Ticket of No Return). Stein is specifically featured in Greta Schiller's 1996 documentary, *Paris Was A Woman* and in Alan Rudolph's 1988 semifictional *The Moderns,* where a rather unflattering depiction of the Stein salon figures memorably. Several more contemporary films look centrally at Stein and Toklas; Perry Miller Adato's *When This You See Remember Me* (1970) and Jill Godmilow's somewhat fanciful *Waiting for the Moon* (1987) offer two examples.

Music, too, bears her influence. Stein has served as the subject of several musical compositions, such as Vivien Fine's *The Women in the Garden* and Virgil Thomson and Georges Hugnet's *The Cradle of Gertrude Stein, or, Mysteries in the Rue de Fleurus.* Through a compact disc accompanying the third issue of *VOYS: A Journal Exploring Sign in Sound* (1998), the words of Stein's "Miss Furr and Miss Skeene," "Not Slightly," and "What Happened" become lyrics and are woven into electronic musical compositions. Stein's signature phrases ("You are all a lost generation," "no there there," "begin again," and "a rose is a rose is a rose") are referenced indirectly in still more popular music, from the lyrics of Don McLean's "American Pie" ("And there we were all in one place / A generation lost in space / With no time left to start again") and R. E. M.'s "Begin the Begin" ("I can't even rhyme / Let's begin the begin") to the title of Aretha Franklin's 1998 release, "A Rose Is Still A Rose."

In keeping with the status some readers accord her as the first postmodernist, Stein also appears on the Internet in numerous forms. Along with interviews and collections of quotations, full texts of at least three of her pieces—"As A Wife Has A Cow A Love Story," *Tender Buttons,* and "Reflections on the Atomic Bomb"—are available there, as are sound clips, biographies, and bibliographies. An online journal, *time-sense: an electronic quarterly on the art of Gertrude Stein,* edited by Sonja Streuber, began in 1998 as a venue for Stein scholarship.[100] In addition, the Gertrude Stein Repertory Theater, headed by Cheryl Faver, has created a "digital salon" dedicated to "building an interactive world stage in real and virtual space and time."[101] Indeed, in the sometimes charming but ever eccentric excess of the Internet, one can even call up a cyber-replica of Stein's American pigeon wallpaper at 5 rue Christine, a photograph of Stein's gravesite in France, or excerpts from Alice B. Toklas's culinary adventures, including "Murder in the Kitchen," in which Toklas likens her interest in cookbooks to Stein's affection for crime stories.

Stein has even lent her name to a well-known if also anonymous voice of protest against racism and sexism in the art world. This cadre of activists, known as the Guerrilla Girls, identify themselves as

> a group of women artists and art professionals who make posters about discrimination. Dubbing ourselves the conscience of the art world, we declare ourselves feminist counterparts to the mostly male tradition of anonymous do-gooders like Robin Hood, Batman, and the Lone Ranger. We wear gorilla masks to focus on the issues rather than our personalities. We use humor to convey information, provoke discussion, and show that feminists can be funny.[102]

The group had its inception after a 1985 exhibition at New York's Museum of Modern Art, bearing the ambitious title "An International Survey of Painting and Sculpture," appeared with a curator's statement from Kynaston McShine that any artist not included in the show should rethink "his" career. The exhibit featured 169 artists. All were white. All were from the United States or Europe. Only 13 were women. In response to this affront "the conscience of the art world" was born. Rather than merely picket or boycott (girlcott?), the Guerrilla Girls, attired in gorilla suits, engage in theatrical interventions and use mass-media forms such as posters, buttons, and stickers to showcase their views. This camp spirit becomes evident in the subtitle of *Confessions of the Guerrilla Girls*: "how a bunch of masked avengers fight sexism and racism in the art world with facts, humor, and fake fur." Responses to their direct actions have also rehearsed the "host" culture's unease with camp and its ways of signifying on the products of the purported cultural mainstream. Hilton Kramer, for instance, is said to have labelled the Guerrilla Girls "Quota Queens." His choice of epithet indicates both a failure of understanding (the Guerrilla Girls have never advocated quotas to achieve representation of artists) and a somewhat phobic reaction to the queer valences of guerrilla theater.

For the purposes of interviews and other situations where it becomes useful to distinguish among guerrilla girls, they adopt the names of dead women artists and writers. One such guerrilla girl, under the name of Gertrude Stein, took the occasion of a group interview to quip that, "There's a popular misconception that the world of High Art is ahead of mass culture but everything in our research shows that, instead of being avant garde, it's derriere" (Guerilla Girls, 26). With their activist zaps, reminiscent in some ways of countercultural happenings, the Guerrilla

Girls reclaim Stein, effectively renaming her as a figure whose agency, like that of the Guerrilla Girls, proceeds from a critical rather than judgmental engagement with cultural forms, both pop and serious, that tempers transgression with humor.

Like other popular icons—Oscar Wilde, Jacqueline Kennedy Onassis, Andy Warhol—Gertrude Stein existed as both a person and a personality. Like Wilde, Onassis, and Warhol, Stein could marshal her poses and manage her publicity, but she could not anticipate or preside over the ways in which and ends toward which others would come to appropriate her image. No public figure really can. These Stein-influenced texts, whether camp, tribute, parody, legacy-building, or derivative forms, bespeak the ways in which Stein has become not only a recovered experimentalist but also something of a pop legend. Although Stein remains an underread modernist, the implication of her work is etched across literature, culture, and art of her time through the present. As this examination of expressive forms outside the academy further demonstrates, Stein's voice and visage permeate today's mass-cultural forms in much the same manner that popular culture pervaded her work, completing a circle of influence, curiosity, and passionate dialogue. The story begins again and again.

Notes to Part 1

1. Gary Schmidgall, *The Stranger Wilde: Interpreting Oscar* (New York: Dutton, 1994), 17.

2. Ellen Berry, "On Reading Gertrude Stein," *Genders* 5 (Summer 1989): 1.

3. Linda Watts, *Rapture Untold: Gender, Mysticism, and 'The Moment of Recognition' in the Writings of Gertrude Stein* (New York: Lang, 1996).

4. Sandra M. Gilbert and Susan Gubar, *No Man's Land: The Place of the Woman Writer in the Twentieth Century* (New Haven, Conn.: Yale University Press, 1989), 245; hereafter cited in text.

5. Marianne DeKoven, "Introduction: Transformations of Gertrude Stein," *Gertrude Stein Issue, Modern Fiction Studies* 42, no. 3 (Fall 1996): 471–72.

6. Gertrude Stein, *Four in America*, with an introduction by Thornton Wilder (New Haven, Conn.: Yale University Press, 1947), 135.

7. Judy Grahn, *Really Reading Gertrude Stein: A Selected Anthology* (Freedom, Calif.: Crossing Press, 1989), 5–6; hereafter cited in text.

8. Harriet Chessman, *The Public Is Invited to Dance: Representation, the Body, and Dialogue in Gertrude Stein* (Stanford, Calif.: Stanford University Press, 1989), 8; hereafter cited in text.

9. Nancy Gray, *Language Unbound: On Experimental Writing by Women* (Chicago: University of Illinois Press, 1992), 46.

10. Jane Palatini Bowers, *Gertrude Stein* (New York: St. Martin's, 1992), 2–3.

11. Lisa Ruddick, "Stein and Cultural Criticism in the Nineties," *Modern Fiction Studies* 42, no. 3 (Fall 1996): 657–58.

12. Henry Sayre, "Performance," in *Critical Terms for Literary Study*, ed. Frank Lentricchia and Thomas McLaughlin (Chicago: University of Chicago Press, 1995), 99.

13. Gertrude Stein, *The Making of Americans: The Hersland Family* (New York: Harcourt, Brace, 1934); hereafter cited in text as *TMOA*.

14. Gertrude Stein, *Blood on the Dining-Room Floor*, with a foreword by Donald Gallup (Pawlet, Vt.: Banyon, 1948); hereafter cited in text as *BDR*.

15. Gertrude Stein, *The World Is Round* (San Francisco: North Point, 1988); hereafter cited in text as *WIR*.

16. Gertrude Stein, "Didn't Nelly and Lilly Love You," in *As Fine as Melanctha*, with a foreword by Nathalie Clifford Barney (New Haven, Conn.: Yale University Press, 1954); hereafter cited in text as *N&L*. The volume in which it appears will hereafter be cited in text as *AFAM*.

17. "Gertrude Stein: A Radio Interview," interview by William Lundell, WJZ and NET, 12 November 1934. Typescript, Gertrude Stein Papers, The Yale Collection of American Literature, Beinecke Rare Book and Manuscript Library, Yale University, New Haven, Conn.

18. Gertrude Stein, "A Long Gay Book," in *Matisse, Picasso, and Gertrude Stein, with Two Shorter Stories* (Boston: Something Else, 1972), 29; hereafter cited in text as LGB.

19. Gertrude Stein, *Everybody's Autobiography* (New York: Cooper Square Publishers, 1971); hereafter cited in text as *EA*.

20. Cynthia Secor, "The Question of Gertrude Stein," in *American Novelists Revisited: Essays in Feminist Criticism*, ed. Fritz Fleischmann (New York: G. K. Hall, 1982), 303.

21. "A Transatlantic Interview—1946," in *A Primer for the Gradual Understanding of Gertrude Stein*, ed. Robert Bartlett Haas (Los Angeles: Black Sparrow, 1971), 22.

22. Clive Bush, *Halfway to Revolution: Investigation and Crisis in the Work of Henry Adams, William James, and Gertrude Stein* (New Haven, Conn.: Yale University Press, 1991), 360, 342.

23. Thorstein Veblen, *The Theory of the Leisure Class* (New York: Dover, 1994).

24. John Preston, "A Conversation with Gertrude Stein," in *Gertrude Stein Remembered*, ed. Linda Simon (Lincoln: University of Nebraska Press, 1994), 165; hereafter cited in text.

25. Shari Benstock, "Expatriate Sapphic Modernism: Entering Literary History," in *Lesbian Texts and Contexts: Radical Revisions*, ed. Karla Jay and Joanne Glasgow (New York: New York University Press, 1990), 198.

26. Gertrude Stein, quoted in William Gass, "Gertrude Stein and the Geography of the Sentence," in *The World within the Word* (New York: Knopf, 1978), 66.

27. Gertrude Stein, *The Geographical History of America or The Relation of Human Nature to the Human Mind*, with an introduction by Thornton Wilder (New York: Random House, 1936), 243; hereafter cited in text as *GHA*.

28. Gertrude Stein, *The Autobiography of Alice B. Toklas* (New York: Vintage Books, 1933); hereafter cited in text as *ABT*; Gertrude Stein, *Four Saints in Three Acts* (New York: Modern Library, 1934).

29. Gertrude Stein, *Narration: Four Lectures by Gertrude Stein*, with an introduction by Thornton Wilder (Chicago: University of Chicago Press, 1935); Gertrude Stein, *How Writing Is Written*, ed. Robert Bartlett Haas (Los Angeles: Black Sparrow, 1974); Gertrude Stein, *How to Write* (Paris: Plain Edition, 1931).

30. F. Richard Thomas, *Literary Admirers of Alfred Stieglitz* (Carbondale: Southern Illinois University Press, 1951).

31. Janet Hobhouse, *Everybody Who Was Anybody: A Biography of Gertrude Stein* (New York: Putnam, 1975), 168; hereafter cited in text.

32. Gertrude Stein to Samuel Steward, February 1940, *Dear Sammy: Letters from Gertrude Stein*, ed. Samuel Steward (Boston: Houghton Mifflin, 1977), 51.

33. Gertrude Stein, *Operas and Plays* (Paris: Plain Edition, 1932); hereafter cited in text as *O&P*.

34. Beth Hutchison, "Gertrude Stein's Film Scenarios," *Literature/Film Quarterly* 17, no. 1 (1989): 35–38.

35. Alice B. Toklas, *What Is Remembered* (New York: Holt, Rinehart, and Winston, 1963), 152.

36. Charles Chaplin, *My Autobiography* (New York: Simon and Schuster, 1964), 306.

37. Ann Douglas, *Terrible Honesty: Mongrel Manhattan in the 1920s* (New York: Farrar, Straus, and Giroux, 1995), 121; hereafter cited in text.

38. Angela Hewett, "The 'Great Company of *Real* Women': Modernist Women Writers and Mass Commercial Culture," in *Rereading Modernism: New Directions in Feminist Criticism*, ed. Lisa Rado (New York: Garland, 1994), 369.

39. Gertrude Stein to Carl Van Vechten, 1 October 1939, *The Letters of Gertrude Stein and Carl Van Vechten*, ed. Edward Burns (New York: Columbia University Press, 1986), 651–52.

40. Andreas Huyssen, *After the Great Divide: Modernism, Mass Culture, Postmodernism* (Bloomington: Indiana University Press, 1986), viii–ix.

41. Ellen Berry, *Curved Thought and Textual Wandering: Gertrude Stein's Postmodernism* (Ann Arbor: University of Michigan Press, 1992), 134.

42. Peter Stallybrass and Allon White, *The Politics and Poetics of Transgression* (Ithaca, N. Y.: Cornell University Press, 1986), 193.

43. Bennett Cerf, *Try and Stop Me* (New York: Simon and Schuster, 1944), 129.

44. Chessman; Alison Rieke, *The Senses of Nonsense* (Iowa City: University of Iowa Press, 1992; Richard Kostelanetz, ed., *Gertrude Stein Advanced: An Anthology of Criticism* (Jefferson, N.C.: McFarland, 1990).

45. Brooks Landon, " 'Not Solve It But Be In It': Gertrude Stein's Detective Stories and the Mystery of Creativity," *American Literature* 53, no. 3 (November 1981): 487–98; Susanne Rohr, " 'Everybody sees, and everybody says they do': Another Guess at Gertrude Stein's *Blood on the Dining-Room Floor,*" *Amerikastudien* 41, no. 4 (1996): 593–602; Jane Detweiler, "A Piano in the Margin: Gertrude Stein 'Detected' in *Blood on the Dining-Room Floor,*" *Kentucky Philological Review* 7 (1992): 12–16.

46. Susannah Radstone, ed., *Sweet Dreams: Sexuality, Gender, and Popular Fiction* (London: Lawrence and Wishart, 1988), 110.

47. Michael Hoffman, *Gertrude Stein* (Boston: Twayne, 1976), 96–97.

48. Bettina Knapp, *Gertrude Stein* (New York: Continuum, 1990), 166.

49. David Dunlap, "For New York's Parks, First Statues of Famous American Women," *New York Times,* 16 July 1992, B1.

50. Gertrude Stein, *Alphabets and Birthdays,* with an introduction by Donald Gallup (Freeport, Maine: Books for Libraries, 1957).

51. Michael Williams, "Mart Trips Mousetrap as French Dis Disney," *Variety,* 1 June 1992, 1, 89.

52. bell hooks discusses "back talk" in her collection of essays *Talking Back: Thinking Feminist, Thinking Black* (Boston: South End, 1989).

53. Marcia Lieberman, " 'Some Day My Prince Will Come': Female Acculturation through the Fairy Tale," in *Gender Images: Readings for Composition,* ed. Melita Schaum and Connie Flanagan (Boston: Houghton Mifflin, 1992), 248–49.

54. Carrie Mae Weems, "Mirror Mirror," in *Mixed Blessings: New Art for a Multicultural Society,* by Lucy Lippard (New York: Pantheon, 1990), 38.

55. Mary Daly discusses re-verse-als and the looking glass society in *Webster's First New Intergalactic Wickedary of the English Language* (Boston: Beacon, 1987), 208; hereafter cited in text.

56. Toni Cade Bambara, ed. *Tales and Stories for Black Folks* (Garden City, N.Y.: Doubleday, 1971); hereafter cited in text.

57. Kristen Wardetzky, "The Structure and Interpretation of Fairy Tales Composed by Children," *Journal of American Folklore* 103 (April/June 1990): 157–77.

58. I borrow the term "woman lore" from Paula Gunn Allen. See *The Sacred Hoop: Recovering the Feminine in American Indian Traditions* (Boston: Beacon, 1986).

59. Bruce Kellner, *A Gertrude Stein Companion: Content with the Example* (Westport, N.Y.: Greenwood, 1988), 69–70; hereafter cited in text.

60. Rachel Blau DuPlessis, *Writing beyond the Ending: Narrative Strategies of Twentieth-Century Women Writers* (Bloomington: Indiana University Press, 1985).

61. Richard Bridgman, *Gertrude Stein in Pieces* (New York: Oxford University Press, 1970), 304; hereafter cited in text.

62. Philip Keith, "How to Write Like Gertrude Stein," in *Audits of Meaning,* ed. Louise K. Smith (Portsmouth, N.H.: Boynton/Cook, 1988), 232.

63. Amal Tracher, "What Is Life without My Love?: Desire and Romantic Fiction," in *Sweet Dreams: Sexuality, Gender, and Popular Fiction,* ed. Susannah Radstone (London: Lawrence and Wishart, 1988), 73.

64. Gertrude Stein, *Lifting Belly,* ed. Rebecca Mark (Tallahassee: NAIAD, 1989); hereafter cited in text as *LB.*

65. Gertrude Stein, *Q.E.D.,* in *"Fernhurst," "Q.E.D.," and Other Early Writings,* ed. Leon Katz (New York: Liveright, 1971).

66. Doris Klaitch, *Woman Plus Woman: Attitudes Toward Lesbianism* (New York: Simon and Schuster, 1974), 207.

67. Gertrude Stein, quoted in *Dear Sammy: Letters from Gertrude Stein,* ed. Samuel Steward (Boston: Houghton Mifflin, 1977), 57.

68. Alice B. Toklas to Carl Van Vechten, 19 April 1947, *Staying On Alone: Letters of Alice B. Toklas,* ed. Edward Burns (Garden City, N.Y.: Liveright, 1973), 62–63.

69. Leon Katz, quoted in Bridgman, 40.

70. Gertrude Stein, "Miss Furr and Miss Skeene," in *A Stein Reader,* ed. Ulla E. Dydo (Evanston, Ill.: Northwestern University Press, 1993).

71. Elizabeth Fifer, *Rescued Readings: A Reconstruction of Gertrude Stein's Difficult Texts* (Detroit, Mich.: Wayne State University Press, 1992), 13.

72. Gertrude Stein, "A Lyrical Opera Made By Two To Be Sung," in *O&P,* 57.

73. Gertrude Stein, "Birth and Marriage," in *Alphabets and Birthdays,* with an introduction by Donald Gallup (Freeport: Books for Libraries, 1957); hereafter cited in text as B&M. Gertrude Stein, "A Sonatina Followed by Another," in *Bee Time Vine and Other Pieces* (Freeport, Maine: Books for Libraries, 1953).

74. Ulla E. Dydo, introduction to "As A Wife Has A Cow A Love Story," in *A Stein Reader,* ed. Ulla E. Dydo (Evanston, Ill.: Northwestern University Press, 1993), 451.

75. Wayne Koestenbaum, "Stein Is Nice," *Parnassus* 20 (1995): 303; hereafter cited in text.

76. Judith Butler, *Gender Trouble: Feminism and the Subversion of Identity* (New York: Routledge, 1990), 31.

77. Sue-Ellen Case, "Toward a Butche-Femme Aesthetic," in *Making a Spectacle: Feminist Essays on Contemporary Women's Theatre,* ed. Lynda Hart (Ann Arbor: University of Michigan Press, 1989), 287.

78. David Bergman, *Camp Grounds: Style and Homosexuality* (Amherst: University of Massachusetts Press, 1993), 4–5; hereafter cited in text.

79. Jack Babuscio, "Camp and the Gay Sensibility," in Bergman, 28; hereafter cited in text as Babuscio.

80. Esther Newton, "Role Models," in Bergman, 46.

81. Philip Core, *Camp: The Lie That Tells the Truth* (New York: Putnam, 1984); hereafter cited in text.

82. Wayne Dynes, ed., *Encyclopedia of Homosexuality* (New York: Garland, 1990), 189; hereafter cited in text.

83. Karl Keller, "Walt Whitman Camping," in Bergman, 114.

84. David Bergman, "Strategic Camp: The Art of Gay Rhetoric," in *Gaiety Transfigured: Gay Self-Representation in American Literature* (Madison: University of Wisconsin Press, 1991), 106.

85. Michael Hoffman, *Critical Essays on Gertrude Stein* (Boston: G. K. Hall, 1986), 39.

86. Gregory Woods, "High Culture and High Camp: The Case of Marcel Proust," in Bergman, 131.

87. Susan Gubar, "Blessings in Disguise: Cross-Dressing and Re-Dressing for Female Modernists," *Massachusetts Review* 22, no. 4 (Autumn 1981): 477–508; hereafter cited in text. Marjorie Garber, *Vested Interests: Cross Dressing and Cultural Anxiety* (New York: Routledge, 1992).

88. Shari Benstock, *Women of the Left Bank* (Austin: University of Texas Press, 1986), 111.

89. Gertrude Stein, *Lectures in America* (New York: Random House, 1935).

90. Susan Sontag, *Against Interpretation and Other Essays* (New York: Farrar, Straus, and Giroux, 1966), 282–83.

91. Corey Creekmur and Alexander Doty, eds., *Out in Culture: Gay, Lesbian, and Queer Essays on Popular Culture* (Durham, N.C.: Duke University Press, 1995), 2.

92. Daniel Harris, *The Rise and Fall of Gay Culture* (New York: Hyperion, 1997).

93. Mary Ellen Haight, *Walks in Gertrude Stein's Paris* (Salt Lake City, Utah: Peregrine Smith Books, 1988).

94. Tom Hachtman, *Fun City* (New York: St. Martin's, 1983).

95. Samuel Steward, *Murder is Murder is Murder* (Boston: Alyson, 1985) and *The Caravaggio Shawl* (Boston: Alyson, 1989).

96. Karren Alenier, *Bumper Cars: Gertrude Said She Took Him for a Ride* (Tempe, Ariz.: Mica Press, 1997).

97. Sarah Strohmeyer and Geoff Hansen, *Barbie Unbound: A Parody of the Barbie Obsession* (Norwich, England: New Victoria Publications, 1997).

98. Bertha Harris, *Gertrude Stein*, Lives of Notable Gay Men and Lesbians (New York: Chelsea House, 1995); Ann LaFarge, *Gertrude Stein*, American Women of Achievement (New York: Chelsea House, 1988); Robert Giard, *Particular Voices: Portraits of Gay and Lesbian Writers* (Cambridge, Mass.: MIT Press, 1988); Jennifer Blessing, *Rrose is a Rrose is a Rrose: Gender Performance in Photography* (New York: Guggenheim Foundation, 1997).

99. Sandra Shotlander, *Framework* (Montmorency, France: Yackandandah Playscripts, 1987), 15.

100. The publication, *time-sense,* can be found on the Internet at <http://www.tenderbuttons.com>.

101. The Gertrude Stein Repertory Theater can be found on the Internet at <http://www.gertstein.org>.

102. Guerrilla Girls Web site can be found at <http://www.guerrillagirls.com>. See also Guerrilla Girls, *Confessions of the Guerrilla Girls* (New York: HarperPerennial, 1995); hereafter cited in text.

Part 2

THE WRITER

Introduction

Gertrude Stein was constantly engaged in commentary on her own work. In the period during and following her trip to lecture in the United States in the 1930s, Stein found herself with new contexts in which to shape that discourse. She not only had a wider audience with which to contend but also found her language and experience cast into new mass-cultural forms—the motion picture, the airplane, the radio broadcast. Stein participated in one radio session that, although thoroughly scripted, was delivered as a live interview. The transcript of that encounter reveals Stein's purported quest for simplicity in her writing, as she defends the work the interviewer finds unintelligible.

Stein had discovered over the years that, to her dismay, people asking about her work—including print journalists—were more interested in her literary salon than her work. During Stein's lecture tour in the United States, she nonetheless granted a number of audiences with the popular press. After the recent success of her gossip-like *Autobiography of Alice B. Toklas,* in which Stein herself appears prominently, it became more difficult to deflect questions about her authorship, including those of a biographical nature. Of this problem, Stein fashioned an opportunity for advertisement. She took the occasion to promote *The Autobiography of Alice B. Toklas* and other works, such as *Portraits and Prayers.*

While in the United States to deliver her lectures, Gertrude Stein gave a number of interviews. Her radio interview with William Lundell, a reporter for NBC, was one such event. Their broadcast took place on 12 November 1934. Both Lundell and Stein had recorded their portions of the interview in advance, rendering the radio session more of a performance/enactment than a live conversation. The exchange with Lundell begins cordially enough, with small talk about her visit to the States. Before long, though, the tone of the interview shifts to more pointed questioning by Lundell and more attenuated, brusque responses from Stein. Indeed, at times the session lapses into an adversarial discourse, and on at least ten instances, Lundell's questions take on the syntax of either rebuttal or disbelief, commencing with

87

"But. . . ." Along the way, Stein shares her impressions of the changed America she found upon her return, fields questions about her libretto for *Four Saints in Three Acts*, describes her composition of the *Autobiography*, and touches on several aspects of her theory of language (both sounded and on the page).

Following the text of Lundell's interview is "All of It," Stein's account of selected experiences on the U.S. tour. She remarks on an America in important ways changed since her departure in 1902. She writes of skyscrapers, New York streets, and city lights as spectacles, as well as more traditional entertainments such as the Yale-Dartmouth football game. Although she struggles between calling her experiences of this rediscovered America "natural" and "strange," the overwhelming sentiment is approving. Still, she finds it peculiar to witness her name in newspapers, her image in photographs, her voice on recordings, and her likeness and voice on newsreels. A memoir of sorts, "All of It" highlights some of Stein's new experiences on the trip, such as air travel. Stein also comments on her experience of the Lundell broadcast, recalling it as a "make-believe" interview. Her alternate title for this text ("I Came and Here I Am"), then, seems to reflect ironically on its historical counterpart (the declaration "I came, I saw, I conquered"), to hint at the sexual innuendo at work in her writing, and to give voice to Stein's disbelief in modern discoveries and the attendant self-estrangement she experiences when encountering mass media representations of herself.

By 1940, just a few years after the lecture tour and interview with Lundell, Stein had lost interest in the rhetorical situation of radio broadcast. She wrote to fellow author Thornton Wilder that "the sound of the human voice over the radio has forever stopped my interest in the problem of the human voice and its relation to the audience."[1] Radio, the form that, as a modern creation, had once tantalized her with the possibility of a new audience, had by then lost its luster. In 1934, however, even the rehearsed nature of the Lundell interview did not obscure Stein's enthusiasm for the new medium.

Also included here is "Why I Like Detective Stories," Stein's tribute to literary sleuths. This text, with its self-explanatory title, sets out Stein's statement of her relationship to the popular literary genre as both a reader and a writer, a consumer and a producer. In this text she identifies her favorite detective writers, such as Edgar Wallace and Sir Arthur Conan Doyle. Stein also comments on her own efforts in response to the detective genre: "Is Dead," "A Piano and a Waterfall," and *Blood on the Dining-Room Floor*. While Stein typically discussed her work with unabashed self-congratulation, it is noteworthy that in "Why I Like Detective Stories" and elsewhere in her writing she finds fault with the texts she refers to as her detective stories. For reasons she does not detail, Stein regarded her work in the detective genre as worthy but flawed attempts.

Throughout these selections, Stein speaks to, through, and back to modern mass-cultural forms of experience.

Note

1. Gertrude Stein to Thornton Wilder, 18 May 1940, in *The Letters of Gertrude Stein and Thornton Wilder,* ed., Edward Burns and Ulla Dydo (New Haven, Conn.: Yale University Press, 1996), 265. Judith Johnston has written about the influence of the gramophone on Stein; see "After the Invention of the Gramophone: Hearing the Woman in Stein's *Autobiography* and Woolf's *Three Guineas,*" in *Virginia Woolf Miscellanies: Proceedings of the First Annual Conference on Virginia Woolf,* ed. Mark Hussey and Vara Neverow-Turk (New York: Pace University Press, 1992).

Gertrude Stein: A Radio Interview

INTERVIEWER: Coming back to the United States for the first time in thirty-one years, Miss Stein, is there anything in particular which has seized your interest?

STEIN: Coming back to the United States after thirty-one years everything seizes my interest and seizes it very hard. The buildings in the air and the people on the street they are all exciting and they are and I know it seems a funny thing to say but that is the way they appeal to me, they are so gentle, so friendly, so simply direct and so sweet. I feel that way about the people on the street and I feel that way about the buildings in the air. By the way what I feel most about the buildings is the way they come down into the earth more than the way they go up into the air and they do it all so naturally and so simply. But the people on the street never could I have imagined the friendly personal simple direct considerate contact that I have with all of them. They all seem to know me and they all speak to me and I who am easily frightened by anything unexpected find this spontaneous considered contact with all and my New York touching and pleasing and I am deeply moved and awfully happy in it. I could tell so many incidents but charming as are the incidents it is the unreality of it the gentle pleasant unreality of it that makes my moving about in the street just a pleasure.

INTERVIEWER: Just yesterday Mr. Cerf told me a story about that, Miss Stein. After the party given in your honor by Random House and the Modern Library, Mr. Cerf going down in the elevator talked with the elevator boy. The boy said, "You had a big party." Mr. Cerf replied "Yes,

"Gertrude Stein: A Radio Interview," interview by William Lundell, WJZ and NET, 12 November 1934. Typescript, Gertrude Stein Papers, The Yale Collection of American Literature, Beinecke Rare Book and Manuscript Library, Yale University, New Haven, Connecticut. © The Estate of Gertrude Stein. Reproduced by permission.

we had all the important celebrities in town. How did it strike you?" The boy said, "Well, I only recognized two of them . . . Miss Stein and Miriam Hopkins, the movie actress."

STEIN: Well, you see the sweet part of that was that we liked each other and asked each other's advice without really knowing who each other was. But in a way that is a joke because what is extraordinary is that in this the largest city in the world everybody knows me and I feel that I know everybody it is just exactly like the village in France where I spend my summers and where there are 20 families and they all know me and I know all of them. Why even at the football game a little boy came up to me and bowed and said please Miss Stein may I have an autograph I said how old are you and he said twelve and we were both pleased, then everybody handed me their programs and it was perfectly charming, simply charming. Why when I first arrived off the boat the first evening I took a walk and I wanted an apple and I went into a little fruit store on sixth avenue to buy it, and the clerk said how do you do Miss Stein did you have a pleasant trip over.

INTERVIEWER: Your coming to the United States to lecture, Miss Stein, seems to me to imply that there are many people who will be able to comprehend your ideas. The current impression of your work, however, among American people is founded largely upon the tremendous publicity attained by *Four Saints in Three Acts*, and although it may seem absurd in them, many American people doubt your ability to speak intelligibly. Just where, then, does *Four Saints in Three Acts* fit into your scheme of lecturing, which, if it is to be successful must be at least understandable . . . which is more than most of us can say for your opera.

STEIN: Look here, being intelligible is not what it seems, after all all these things are a matter of habit. Take what the newspapers say about what you call the New Deal. If you just know ordinary English you do not have the slightest idea what the newspapers are talking about everybody has their own English and it is only a matter of anybody getting used to an English anybody's English and then it is all right. After all when you say they do not understand *Four Saints* what do you mean, of course they understand or they would not listen to it. You mean by understanding that you can talk about it in the way that you have the habit of talking . . . putting it in other words . . . but I mean by understanding enjoyment. If you go to a football game you don't have to understand it in any way except the football way and all you have to do with *Four Saints* is to enjoy it in the *Four Saints* way which is the way I am, otherwise I would not have written it in that way. Don't you see what I mean? If you enjoy it you understand it, and lots of people have enjoyed it so lots of people have understood it. You see that is what my lectures are to be. They are to be a simple way of telling everybody this thing, that if you enjoy it you understand it and so if I am telling them this about why my punctuation is, why my so-called repetition is, what my prose is and what my poetry is and what my plays are and what my English literature is and what my pictures are and I am telling them all this simply as I tell everything you will see, they will understand it because they enjoy it.

INTERVIEWER: Your life has been amazingly full of interest, it would seem Miss Stein judging from *The Autobiography of Alice B. Toklas.*

STEIN: Yes, my life has been and is full of interest because I like it all it is all wonderful to me and one is not more wonderful than the other anybody anybody meets is wonderful and that is all there is to it and if you are wonderful and they are wonderful the world is full of interest and that is natural enough. In *The Autobiography of Alice B. Toklas* I told all this one way, in *Portraits and Prayers* the book that is coming out and I am so pleased that it is coming out just as I am here I have told what it is in another way. You see in *Portraits and Prayers* are collected together all the portraits that I have made of anyone over all these years and what I mean by a portrait is this. When I know anybody well they are all something to me each one is. That is natural but then there has to come a moment when I know all I can know about anyone and I know it all at once and then I try to put it down to put down on paper all that I know of anyone their ways the sound of their voice the accent of their voice their other movements their character all what they do and to do it all at once is very difficult. Just anybody try to do it and you will see what I mean and in this book *Portraits and Prayers* I have tried to do it and I have done it in a great many ways and sometimes I have felt that I have done it. And you must not think that you do not understand because you cannot say it to yourself in other words. If you have something happen in you when you read these portraits you do understand no matter what you say to yourself and others about not understanding. Really and truly that is really and truly true.

INTERVIEWER: As you look back, Miss Stein over these friends of whom you have done portraits, do any Americans stand out from among those told about in *The Autobiography of Alice B. Toklas* and in your latest book, *Portraits and Prayers*?

STEIN: Yes, there are Americans in this book. There is everybody in this book everybody that has been in my life because after anybody has become very well known to me I have tried to make a portrait of them well I might almost say in order to get rid of them inside in me. Otherwise I would have got too full up inside me with what I had inside me of anyone. Do you see what I mean? Yes, there [are] lots of Americans in *Portraits and Prayers* and some of my favorite portraits in it are Americans, there is the second portrait of Carl Van Vechten, and there is one of Sherwood Anderson which I consider perhaps the best portrait I ever did and there is a little one of Hemingway and some of Americans you do not know and another one of an American I loved very much Mildred Aldrich of the Hilltop on the Marne which is there as *Mildred Aldrich Saturday*.

INTERVIEWER: Going back for a moment to your opera to be sung, *Four Saints in Three Acts*—I should like to ask if you sincerely believe that English literature can in any way be improved by such experimentation as you have made in *Four Saints in Three Acts*?

STEIN: There is no question of improving English literature there is only a question of English literature going on and now American literature going on and I do think that my work and *Four Saints in Three Acts* is an important part of it, is an important very important element in English literature's going on and naturally anybody who wants anything wants it to go on and my writing is part of its going on that is the way I feel about it.

INTERVIEWER: I'd like you to speak perfectly frankly, Miss Stein. What do you think of the writing now being done in the United States?

STEIN: The writing in the United States is going on and the young ones send me lots of manuscripts and a great many of them really know what writing is but you see what is necessary is that they should go on writing. Horace Greeley said about the resumption of specie payments after the Civil War that the only way to resume is to resume and that is the way with writing. The only way to go on writing is to go on writing and if you have anything in you it will be something but if you have not it will not but as there is undoubtedly a great deal in America that stirs me a lot coming here there will undoubtedly be a great deal in future American writing.

INTERVIEWER: While reading *The Autobiography of Alice B. Toklas*, Miss Stein, I had an unusual reading experience because of your peculiar style, the words seemed to fly before my eyes. I read page after page with a kind of breathless haste. Just what in your style is responsible for this swiftness?

STEIN: The style of *The Autobiography of Alice B. Toklas*, Mr. Lundell, is not peculiar at all. The only peculiar thing is that I wrote it myself. I suggested to my secretary Alice B. Toklas that she write her life story and she put it off and finally to encourage her one day I sat down in the garden and wrote a chapter then it seized me so I kept on writing and writing sitting in the garden writing and I wrote the whole *Autobiography* in six weeks.

INTERVIEWER: And you didn't go over it to correct it at all?

STEIN: I did not—I just wrote it.

INTERVIEWER: But, Miss Stein, why did you omit capital letters so frequently and question marks?

STEIN: Because capital letters and question marks are useless. They are hangovers from the days when people didn't read very well, that all goes into the whole question of life and death of punctuation marks, if you don't know a question without a question mark what is the use of writing the question?

INTERVIEWER: You mean that question marks and capital letters are crutches for the mentally crippled?

STEIN: That is it exactly they are a help to some people but the average reading mind does not need them.

INTERVIEWER: But in addition to punctuation you seem to have very definite opinions about nouns and adjectives.

STEIN: I do nouns are pretty dead and adjectives which are related to nouns which are practically dead are even more dead.

INTERVIEWER: But where is the life then in writing. In the verb?

STEIN: In the verbs there is life in the prepositions and adverbs too and very much in the conjunctions. As an example the most vigorous expression in American speech is that composed of two words—"And how." It is full of emotion and it says everything that needs to be said.

INTERVIEWER: But your study in these slang phrases it would seem to me must be rather limited. In your literary circles you don't meet much new and vigorous slang.

STEIN: Oh, don't I. Whom did I talk to during the war? And every day I talk to my cab drivers and my publishers.

INTERVIEWER: You apparently find American speech very vigorous then?

STEIN: Oh, yes. American speech is very vigorous, more vigorous than English. English speech is dead and if the speech of the people is dead then the literature is dead. When a country is in transition and growing its speech is vigorous and its literature is vigorous and alive. In the Elizabethan days that was a most lively period and the language was growing and the language was vigorous.

INTERVIEWER: Would that then mean, Miss Stein, that because of the vigor of Greek life in the days of Sophocles and of Roman life in the days of the Caesars that Greek and Latin are not dead languages but very much alive?

STEIN: Certainly they are alive. The literature of any language that was once alive is never dead but the English of modern writers is not in a state of vitality. Since the death of Swinburne, Browning and Meredith there have been no first rate writers in English, just second and third rate and that isn't anybody's fault but England's has lost its vitality.

INTERVIEWER: But what of our younger American writers?

STEIN: Young writers are young writers, you can't judge a writer until all of his work is behind him.

INTERVIEWER: But then how are we to know what books to buy and what is the value of a book reviewer if we can't judge an author's value until his work is finished?

STEIN: The function of a book reviewer is to review and that is alright.

INTERVIEWER: Well, then, to get back to your own writing again, Miss Stein. Will you explain the passage from *Four Saints in Three Acts* about the pigeons on the grass which begins, "Pigeons on the grass alas, pigeons on the grass, alas, short longer grass short longer longer shorter

95

yellow grass," and ends up, "Lily lily Lily let Lily Lucy Lucy let Lily. Let Lucy Lily."

STEIN: That is simple I was walking in the gardens of the Luxembourg in Paris it was the end of summer the grass was yellow I was sorry that it was the end of summer and and [*sic*] I saw the big fat pigeons in the yellow grass and I said to myself, pigeons on the yellow grass, alas, and I kept on writing pigeons on the grass, alas, short longer grass short longer longer shorter yellow grass pigeons large pigeons on the shorter longer yellow grass, alas pigeons on the grass, and I kept on writing until I had emptied myself of the emotion. If a mother is full of her emotion toward a child in the bath the mother will talk and talk and talk until the emotion is over and that's the way a writer is about an emotion.

INTERVIEWER: But how is the reader supposed to know what you are thinking about?

STEIN: The reader does know because he enjoys it. If you enjoy you understand if you understand you enjoy. What you mean by understanding is being able to turn it into other words but that is not necessary. As I said before, to like a football game is to understand it in the football way.

INTERVIEWER: You saw the Yale-Dartmouth game a week ago Saturday, didn't you? Did you understand that in the American way or the football way or how?

STEIN: The thing that interested me was that the Modern American in his movements and his actions in a football game so resembled the red Indian dance and it proves that the physical country that made the one made the other and that the red Indian is still with us. They just put their heads down solemnly together and then double over while on the side lines the substitutes move in a jiggly way just like Indians . . . Then they all get down on all fours just like Indians.

INTERVIEWER: But those jiggles are warming-up exercises.

STEIN: It doesn't make any difference what they are doing it for, they are just like the way the Indian jiggles in the Indian dance and then there is that little brown ball they all bend down and worship.

INTERVIEWER: But the ideas in that is to get the ball across the goal line.

STEIN: But don't you suppose I know that, and don't you suppose the Indians had just as much reason and enjoyed their dancing just as much?

INTERVIEWER: Perhaps so. But permit me, Miss Stein, to ask you to explain the lines entitled *A Portrait of Carl Van Vechten.* I don't understand them. Will you read them.
STEIN: "If it and as if it, if it or as if it, if it is as if it, and it is as if it and as if it. Or as if it. As more. As more as if it. And if it. And for and as if it." That is a portrait of Carl Van Vechten. He is just like that sometimes this way sometimes that way he is sometimes very real and then very unreal sometimes alive sometimes not alive.

INTERVIEWER: But what about this fifth paragraph?
STEIN: "Tied and untied and that is all there is about it. And as tied and as beside, and as beside and tied. Tied and untied and beside and as beside and as untied and as tied and as untied and as beside." Well, just look at the words, the words look like Carl Van Vechten, anybody can know that beside they mean Carl Van Vechten anybody can know that.

INTERVIEWER: Well, that's rather hard for us normal Americans to see.
STEIN: What is a normal American there are lots quite normal who do see. And how. But after all you must enjoy my writing and if you enjoy it you understand it. If you did not enjoy it why do you make a fuss about it? There is the real answer.

All of It

Before coming away from France I did not meditate on being about to visit my native land. If I had meditated on being about to visit my native land I would have been frightened badly frightened and as I do not like to be frightened do not like to be badly frightened I did not meditate on being about to visit my native land.

Then there was the boat.

The boats that is being on the boat is very different than it was being on the boat thirty-one years ago. It is thirty-one years ago, and when I went to buy some fruit on Seventh Avenue on first arriving the man said to me I know you by your picture you are the lady who has not been here for thirty-one years.

Well I had not I had n[o]t been here for thirty-one years, and the boat was very different. This the boat was so like a nice quiet hotel that you did not know unless you wanted to know that you were on a boat. So I was busy about being on the boat and so I did not meditate on being about to visit my native land. And this was just as well, because, well it would not have had anything to do any meditations I might have meditated would have nothing to do, nothing at all to do with what happened.

And then there were the reporters, well I have seen often seen reporters not so many of them but still reporters very nice reporters, and so although there were a good many of them they were all natural enough. And then we landed.

And then it began as it has been going on beginning that is my doing everything that I had never done before. I did not, do not imagine that it is possible to do and keep on doing so many things all the time that I had never done before.

Gertrude Stein, "All of It." Typescript, Gertrude Stein Papers, The Yale Collection of American Literature, Beinecke Rare Book and Manuscript Library, Yale University, New Haven, Connecticut. © The Estate of Gertrude Stein. Reproduced by permission.

And doing something every day and sometimes twice and three times every days seizes my interest and seizes it very hard.

The thing I expected to have bother me does not bother me at all and that is that everybody understands and speaks English, after so many years of being where nobody spoke or understood the language I spoke, I thought that would be an awful worry to me, it was a worry to me the only time I was in England but here the American English tones in with everything and is is so low keyed and it is not something of which I am ever conscious except as a pleasant background. That was an immense surprise to me and the first thing that made me feel that the thing the most persistent thing about New York is its gentleness, its pleasant gentle gentleness. Its beauty and it is beautiful is more apart. What is and it is astonishing beyound words to me that it is what is and what is it is gentle.

As I say we landed and it was all strange and it was all natural, and I am still a good deal that way about it, it is all strange and it is all natural, the little lights such pretty little lights on top of the taxis, and then the strange shapes of the trucks. [T]hese were the things that struck me as we drove up.

And then everything began. It began the doing everything all the time everything that I had never done before n[o]t only not done but never really known was done.

And here we are.

As Stieglitz said when he asked me how I felt about it I suppose it is to you just a continuous Christmas tree and he is right.

And the Christmas tree is a Christmas tree for me and that is a very Christmas thing to be.

Once more what happened, everything happened and it was everything that had never happened to me.

It is very difficult I know for any one to know that living as I was living in Paris, I had never seen or heard a talking cinema, I had never listened to a radio, I had never been near an airplane, I had never for many years been in a train, I had just been at home working and talking and walking. I drove my car from Paris to the country home every spring and back again to Paris every fall and in between nothing much was happening, a great deal inside but never outside, the most exciting was when a dog was sick or we had to change a servant and get a new one. All these things were exciting to me but really nothing really was ever happening but what does happen in ordinary every day living, and now, and how,

Part 2

As I say I arrived and it was very exciting and then all of a sudden the place that is the hotel was filled with everything. It seemed to be all full of something, and the first thing I knew I really cannot say I knew it, before I was doing it, lights were going and there I was sitting and they said will you read something now something from your writing. I did. I would have done anything just then, anything that I had never done before and I did this thing. What was it, I asked as I did docilely anything they told me to do. A news reel they said for Pathe. I knew about them in Paris, that is they had been there when cinemas were first commencing, so of course I did what I was told.

A couple of days later I was told that it was being shown in a theatre, I did not really believe it, I do not know that I quite wanted to believe it anyway I did not go to see or hear it. And then the Pathe people wanted to do another one and they asked me to go and see it, I did. It was awful[.] That is awful to me. I do not suppose anybody who hears all about it can understand, but it was like a second Saint Therese in the opera, I realise now it might have been a shock to the first Saint Therese to have a second Saint Therese. It was a shock to me. It is a shock to one much as one is used to it to see one's name unexpectedly printed in a book or in a newspaper, it happens often but even so every time you see it is a little a startle to you, a slight fright and then a pleasure to you. But to see the whole of yourself and your voice it was more than a fright and a startle the same thing but so much more. That was very much one of the things that had never before been done by me or happened to me.

But to come back to the daily life in New York the pleasant gentle daily life in New York. Never never could any one tell me that the daily life of the streets of New York are what they are. Everybody knows you and you know anybody at least and anyway that is the way it is for me. In my quarter in Paris, everybody knows me and I know everybody, I have seen them as babies and children and grown up men and women, and most of them have lived and do live there all the time as I do. As I know them all and they all speak to me and I always speak to them. And all that is true in the country in Bilignin, of course that is a perfectly natural thing. But that this should be true of the biggest and the most terrifying city in the world that is an astonishing thing, and even now that I know it it is as unreal as it is real and as real as it is unreal.

What do they say to me, well they say any natural thing to me just as I say any natural thing to them. It is strange so very strange that it should be happening as it is happening but the thing itself and the doing of it is all so natural as natural as anything.

The first thing that happened, was in the evening the first evening we went out, I wanted to buy an apple and we went into a store to buy one. How do you Miss Stein said the clerk pleasantly, did you have a good trip. Yes I said just as I might have said it in my own Paris quarter and we went on talking, it was only gradually that I thought it was funny that he should have known me, it was all done in such a natural way. That is the way it began and that is the way it has been going on ever since. What do they say to me and what do I say to them, why everything that is perfectly natural for them to say to me and perfectly natural for me to say to them, when you stop and talk to any of them. And that is the astonishing the completely wholly astonishing thing about all America that it is so naturally that thing.

That makes it different from anything else and makes me know that after all I am American, it is so completely entirely and particularly a natural thing everything that is American, it is so natural that it is like being in a dream an active dream.

To go on with everything happening, of course there was the lecturing that is what I came for but I will tell about that last and then there was the airplane, that was very exciting. I never had lectured to or done any of that. And the first thing I did about it was to be photographed with it without doing it, and then I heard it without doing it and now I am going to be doing it.

Why I Like Detective Stories

Life said Edgar is neither long nor short, and anybody knows that the only detective stories that anybody can read are written by Edgar. When Gerald Berners was here and his chauffeur William they both wanted detective stories, I gave William Edgar Wallace, he wanted Edgar Wallace, I cannot say that Gerald Berners did, but then he might have, anyway I had them to give them and I always find a new one by him, you might think other people wrote them but finally you know better, you finally do know that all the Edgar Wallace stories are written by him.

What are detective stories, well detective stories are what I can read. You are always finding a new author and each one makes you very enthusiastic, and then you get used to it and on the whole like to read them over again, there are the Coles and Farjeon. Farjeon is very good, he tries to be as good as Edgar Wallace but in a kind of a way it is always a mistake to try. On the whole I think English ones better than American ones, they are more long winded which is better and money is more real in them which is very much better.

Here is a little conversation about them. It is called *Money Is Not Money.*

Money is not money said Edgar to Edgar. What do you mean by that said Edgar, I mean by that said Edgar that money is not money if you do not owe money to another. Oh yes yes said Edgar. But you always do you do always owe money to another, no said Edgar. No.

It was Thursday and they said this to each other on Thursday. On Friday they said it again, Edgar said that money is not money if you do not have to give money to somebody else. Suppose said Edgar you owe yourself money then it is not money, oh yes it is said Edgar. Edgar did not listen to Edgar because he knew better than Edgar.

Gertrude Stein, "Why I Like Detective Stories," *Harper's Bazaar,* November 1937, 70, 104, 106. Gertrude Stein Papers, The Yale Collection of American Literature, Beinecke Rare Book and Manuscript Library, Yale University, New Haven, Connecticut. © The Estate of Gertrude Stein. Reproduced by permission.

So then Saturday came and then Sunday. Edgar went out in the evening, he had been out in the afternoon and he went out in the evening. So did Edgar. They met and they talked together and they talked about it, Edgar said I tell you money is not money if you do not owe it to another, now he said listen, a father of course if he has children he is a father, a father if he stops the allowance of his children the children if they have to spend it have to get it and so they get it from their father. You see said Edgar children cannot steal from their father that is french law, a father cannot accuse his children of stealing from him not according to french law so if the father does not give the money to his children then the children can take it from the father and it is not money until they pay it to someone else. That is what Edgar said to Edgar and after that Edgar said that they need hours to think about that and then they settled to go away. Edgar went and after that Edgar went away. It made them go one at a time.

You see that is the reason why money has to be, otherwise a detective story could not be interesting. Edgar Wallace makes it mysterious but it is always money, it is a disappointment when it is drugs or an international conspiracy, you always have the feeling that all the struggle is not worth while because by the time the real war comes all that diplomacy will have been forgotten and so what is the use and drugs that is the same, just about the same quantity of drugs get in anyway, but money that is different, twenty guineas is different, money is different and English people do feel that money is more real than Americans feel it is and that is why their detective stories are so much more soothing.

I used to think that a detective story was soothing because the hero being dead, you begin with the corpse you did not have to take him on and so your mind was free to enjoy yourself, of course there is the detection but nobody really believes in detection, that is what makes the detection so soothing, they try to make you believe in the detection by trying to make you fond of the character that does the detecting, they know if you do not get fond of him you will not believe in the detection, naturally not and you have to believe in it a little or else it will not be soothing. I like detecting there are so many things to detect, why did somebody say what they said, why did somebody cut out a paragraph in the proof I was correcting, why did the young man we were to meet at the station and whom we have never seen before not turn up and why did they telephone to somebody else that he was still at the station waiting for us and why when we got there could nobody find him neither the fat porter nor the thin one and certainly it was a very small station finally why when we had all given him up and we were starting for home did I find him on the other side of the station and where had he been. He never did tell us but I detected the reason it was because he resembled some one else who might have done it although the other one never had.

Really why Edgar Wallace is so good is that there is no detection. He makes it ordinary and the ordinary because he is genuinely romantic has an extraordinary charm. The girl will always be caught by the villain just before the end and the chase is to end only in one way that is in the rescue and sometimes he has to cudgel his brains to find some reason for this capture of the heroine but captured she is and it is a charm. Moreover and of course that is the important moreover there can be in any of his books lots of them lots of everybody but there does not ever have to be a dead one it is like a good play of Shakespeare, have them dead but if they are dead then the place is strewn with corpses, but and that is the real reason why Edgar Wallace holds is because his books are strewn with people with plans with everything as well as with corpses there is a genuine abundance and the thing that can be said is characteristic of the twentieth century is that it is lavish but niggardly. Oppenheim is that but Edgar Wallace never, from the first *People of the River* to the last chase for the girl there is abundance, of course incidentally he writes awfully well he has the gift of writing as Walter Scott had it and that too makes for abundance. I like Edgar Wallace. For many years his sadism put me off as Dickens' sadism put me off but finally you have to conclude that English abundance has to have that and alright I like abundance.

They say that there are an awful lot of detective stories written but really there are not really not, if you want to read one a day well not one a day but one every other day, say three a week and if you are willing to read over and over a lot of them even then there are not enough to go around if you include English and American ones, really there are not I can say in all sincerity that there are not.

I tried to write one well not exactly write one because to try is to cry but I did try to write one.

It had a good name it was *Blood on the Dining-Room Floor* and it all had to do with that but there was no corpse and the detecting was general, it was all very clear in my head but it did not get natural, the trouble was that if it all happened and it all had happened then you had to mix it up with other things that had happened and after all a novel even if it is a detective story ought not to mix up what happened with what has happened, anything that has happened is exciting exciting enough without any writing, tell it as often as you like but do not write it not as a story.

However I did write it, it was such a good detective story but nobody did any detecting except just conversation so after all it was not a detective story so finally I concluded that even although Edgar Wallace does almost write detective stories without anybody really doing any detecting on the whole a detective story has to have if it has not a detective it has to have an ending and my detective story did not have any.

I was sorry about it because it came so near to being a detective story and it did have a good title. Anyway finally I did write two very little ones, all about the same time, one was called *A Piano and a Waterfall* the other one was called *Is Dead*, but there was no detective hero there were corpses but no detecting and there was money but that was there completely separated from what had been happening, if you have no motive and no detecting can it be a detective story I can only hope so because I would really and truly like to write one.

And so it comes to this the best detective story writer Edgar Wallace does not really have any detecting and it does not begin with a corpse, there are often plenty of corpses or nearly corpses but they are usually incidental corpses, the really important people come to be corpses sometime but not necessarily while you are reading, most generally not, the only thing you have to do in an Edgar Wallace story is to detect the villain, the villain naturally is a criminal but that is only incidental he is a villain entirely but that is entirely a different thing, and the hero is nothing but a hero, his detecting is incidental and heroine is a heroine because inevitably there is a rescue. Edgar Wallace quite rightly uses the old melodrama machinery and he makes it alive again and that is everything, it is much better to make an old thing alive than to invent a new one anybody can know that.

So then there seems to be only two things to do one of the two things, you either use the old melodrama scheme or you use the Sherlock Holmes super-detective and the crime and the criminal is nothing but something for the unreal hero to conquer, I do not wish to be ungrateful to the Sherlock Holmes kind but I guess I do like the melodrama best, the melodrama scheme gives more abundance than the one hero kind. In the melodrama the three are equal the villain the hero and the heroine, in this order as to importance but nevertheless they all three have the right to be but in the detective hero type the rest of it becomes too dependent and eventually the hero detective having really to exist all by himself ceases to exist at all. I am not ungrateful for that kind I like them but there it is they do have that failing.

There are also the detective stories of Fletcher, there it all depends not upon the criminal not upon the detecting but upon the crime, and the crime is money money is there sometimes as diamonds mostly uncut sometimes cut but it all depends entirely upon the crime, crime and ancient history which explains the crime, here there is neither hero nor villain and certainly not a heroine there is only the crime.

It is funny that crime is soothing but it is, stories of adventure criminals, the kind they used to write about Australian bushrangers were more likely to frighten you than crimes of criminals, I do not know why but this is so. Criminal crimes are soothing, adventure crimes are frightening, I suppose because criminal crimes take place where there are lots of people and adventure crimes take place where there are none. Anyway I do like detective stories and will there please will there be more of them.

Part 3

THE CRITICS

Introduction

The final section of this volume is devoted to reprinting of insightful contemporary Stein criticism. Since the century began, Stein's readers have sought out one another in their efforts to engage the writer's unconventional texts. The process of reader collaboration has continued, and with every passing decade, readers reinvent themselves according to their own textual desires and shifting theories of Stein's work.

Albert Mobilio's piece, "The Lost Generator: Gertrude Stein Builds a Better Reader," addresses the renegotiated contract between reader and writer. Mobilio observes that Stein has functioned as a cultural icon; much of this public persona is the direct result of Stein's acts of self-promotion. According to Mark Booth, author of *Camp*, most key figures of camp have been noteworthy for their abilities in self-promotion, so Stein is in good company.[1]

Referencing Stein's literary biography, Mobilio uses her early works of fiction, including *Things As They Are* (also published as *Q.E.D.*), *Three Lives*, and *The Making of Americans*, to articulate his theory that Stein's work created a system of literary reference centered around Stein herself. Consequently, Stein even claimed for herself the role of literary critic of her work. He further contends that Stein, by thwarting formulaic reading practices, mobilizes readers to collaborate—both with her and with other readers—in constituting experiences of her unconventional texts.

Notes

1. Mark Booth, *Camp* (New York: Quartet Books, 1983).

Albert Mobilio

We first know her as an icon: the sharply sculpted, masklike face hover
ing above the piled upon folds of her body. Her head tilts slightly forward to catch an unnaturally harsh light. Her eyes are askew; one is
indifferently wide, the other squints in judgement. Depicting an unset-
tled Buddha who seems both at rest and about to rise from her over-
stuffed chair, Picasso's portrait of Gertrude Stein is, perhaps, the most
familiar emblem of the Modernist epoch. We can hardly look at this
painting and not imagine, standing just outside the frame, Braque,
Apollinaire, Matisse, Pound, Hemingway, assorted Futurists, Dadaists,
and Cubists—all those who made the art that made this century. Stein
appears enthroned, a high priestess presiding over her charmed circle at
27 Rue de Fleurus. Inevitably, the grand scene the portrait conjures—
Paris in the teens and '20s, the Lost Generation—obscures its subject.
While we view her as a pivotal, even essential participant in the artistic
turmoil of her times, it is always in relation to her legendary salon, her
role as hostess. Yet it was Stein, among all her guests, who truly exe-
cuted the letter of the Modernist law to "make it new." She did this in
some 40 books that leave no genre untouched. Whether as librettist,
poet, novelist, or essayist, Stein consistently produced work so radical it
remains so today. Sadly, this achievement too little informs what we see
when we see Stein. Regarded more as an icon than an artist, more apho-
rist than author, she is our century's most famous unread writer.

Stein lacks readers not merely because the writing is difficult but
because it is, at times, literally unreadable; that is, she cannot be read
the way we've been taught, the way we want to read. She sought to reinvent the relationship between reader and page. Arriving in New York to
lecture in 1934, she made her intent plain to a group of inquiring news-
men. Surprised by the clarity of her responses, one asked, "Why don't

Albert Mobilio, "The Lost Generator: Gertrude Stein Builds a Better Reader,"
Voice Literary Supplement 69 (November 1988): 7–13. © Albert Mobilio.
Reprinted by permission.

you write the way you talk?" "Why don't you read the way I write?" she replied. Doing that means unlearning the fluid rapidity and instantaneous assimilation we automatically bring to bear. We are sent back to our earliest experiences with written words, when their size, shape, and sound were as consequential as the information they conveyed. By tearing at the seams between sentences, between words, Stein invites readers to join in an almost physical act; she forces the eye to retrace, the mind to rethink. Unraveling one of her commaless run-on sentences can resemble a tug-of-war in which Stein pulls you heedlessly forward while you dig in your heels with imagined commas, colons, and periods. Stein unnerves us; she contorts what we think is the natural flow. The violation of so many conventions upends the implicit contract between writer and reader. In place of that neatly struck bargain, Stein insists her readers read recklessly, with no hands on the wheel and a busy eye on the words ahead:

> *I want readers so strangers must do it. Mostly no one knowing me can like it that I love it that every one is of a kind of men and women, that always I am looking and comparing and classifying of them, always I am seeing their repeating, it may be irritating to hear from them but always more and more I love it of them.*

The going can be, by turns, tedious, tiring, or a heady thrill. Much in the way that Schoenberg's unchromatic 12-tone compositions disturb listeners, Stein jangles our ears. Too often her reputation for difficulty has cut short attempts to turn some actual pages. The notion that reading Stein is an unrewarding chore abides, curiously enough, even among her most likely audience—fans of women's and avant literature. The notoriety dates back to the early teens, when Stein published *Portrait of Mabel Dodge* and *Tender Buttons*. These experiments in non-representational prose inspired satirists and provoked critics to extravagant condemnations. (As Stein struggled to find publishers, *Tender Buttons* was parodied in *Life*.) Believed to be something of a great Sphinx writing solely in repetitive riddles and double-talk, Stein seemed to epitomize the Post-Romantic author's dilemma of recreating an intensely private language as public voice. The consensus held that she didn't turn the trick, and she became a byword for Modernist and avant-garde excess.

True enough, Stein flouted grammatical convention, reveled in obscure personal reference, and produced books of daunting length, but how did she differ from Joyce and Pound? Modernist monuments like *Finnegans Wake* and the *Cantos*, never candidates for beach reading, have been treated since their publication, to exhaustive (and exhausting) attention. Stein, on the other hand, has been ridiculed or ignored for the same sins. (Witness the recent flap over editing errors in the new edition of *Ulysses* while *The Making of Americans* remains out of print.) Stein's eccentricities appeared to be willful and self-indulgent, the products of a wealthy dilettante's proximity to real genius. Of course, her male counterparts wielded a purposeful obscurity and bent the rules for only the best of reasons—as a woman, Stein couldn't muster quite the same tolerance from critics. But there's a more telling difference. For as much as innovators like Joyce and Pound wore the mantle of the new, they played a game as old as the Talmud. If you have the right education and access to a good library, reading their "difficult" books amounts to solving an elaborate crossword puzzle. The allusions may be complex, but the hierarchical roles of author as master locksmith and reader as forger of keys remain unchanged. Stein stood resolutely outside this comfy arrangement. She presented the reader an open-ended game in which interpretations were presumed to be private and always in flux. In the absence of fixed symbols writ large, she devised truly free-form texts that converted readers into writers.

The blurred distinction between reader and writer follows from Stein's belief that writing is simply a way of knowing. In the essay "Sentences," she locates the source of what's written. "A sentence can be in one. A sentence in one sentence has been in one. It has been one." Translation—logos is within, in fact, it defines your being. The writer uncovers what's already penned. To call Stein's broken-stride style idiosyncratic is to misjudge its decidedly universal aims. She wanted to capture the rhythms of thinking, an Ur-beat that could be found in "the everlasting feeling of sentences as they diagram themselves." Stein's spiraling sentences mimic the unstoppable quality of thought; she means to draw us deeply in. Her intentionally abbreviated line—"A sentence made slowly"—suggests by its very condensation that the time it takes to write a sentence should equal the time it takes to comprehend it. Consequently, her ideal reader inhabits her sentences' production and reenacts the summing of their parts. This reader surrenders to the jagged pulse of a record being played at variable speeds and is eventually surprised at how right it sounds. If there is a deep grammar, Stein tapped the vein. By stripping the habitual from our sentence-making and reading, she revealed a circularly logical, lucidly incantatory speech, an atavistic tongue flowing just beneath the finely built phrases. Its grammar is the grammar of first speech, the motion and sound are those of human thought.

By agreement, Stein's German-Jewish parents had five children, but two deaths in infancy permitted the births of Leo and Gertrude. A sense of precariousness and unease over owing their lives to the deaths of their siblings would always trouble them both. The family's wanderings did little to encourage feelings of security. By the time Gertrude was seven, the Steins had lived in Pennsylvania, Vienna, Paris, and Baltimore before settling in Oakland. These uprootings made keener the isolation she experienced as the family's youngest. Although pampered and indulged, she was often left to herself or in the company of Leo. She weathered the chaotic procession of languages—acquiring a child's smattering of French and German—but found in the use of English a private pleasure, as if it were her true home. Her choice to live in Europe among foreign languages would replicate the childhood world in which she was "all alone with English and myself."

Neither parent did much to temper her estrangement. Her mother, who died when Stein was 14, was a marginal presence, "never important to her children excepting to begin them." Her father loomed large as an impatient, argumentative, sometimes tyrannical figure. While mothers appear infrequently in Stein's writing, domineering fathers proliferate. Indeed, Daniel Stein, fictionalized as David Hersland in *The Making of Americans*, is the most vivid and passionately drawn of all her characters. Certainly he soured her on fathers for good, so much so that she could later link Hitler, Stalin, Roosevelt, and Mussolini through the common denominator of patriarchy: "There is too much fathering going on just now and there is no doubt about it fathers are depressing." Instead, she cleaved to Leo. Bound by the similar circumstances of their conception, they also shared an attitude of superiority toward the rest of the family. She followed him to Harvard, Johns Hopkins, and Europe, hewing to each of his many turns of mind. Snobbishly brilliant and self-obsessed, Leo Stein thrived on the intensity of intellectual pursuit as well as his own neuroses. He was in thrall to one mentor after another—William James, Matisse, Freud—always measuring himself against them, only to be found wanting. What he called his "pariah complex" condemned him to a cycle of hero worship and frustration. Eventually, in despair over his continued failure and her first successes, he turned his withering condescension on his sister, destroying a bond that had endured for 30 years. Nonetheless, Gertrude was undoubtedly enriched by his aggressive curiosity. Leo furnished her with his style of imperious conviction (which she would leaven with wit) and introduced her to the people who would help supply the convictions.

Stein entered Radcliffe in the mid-1890s and, like Leo, enlisted as one of William James's most avid students. James admitted her to his graduate seminar, where she studied the nature of consciousness and its relation to human behavior. Not just James but many professors and fellow students were impressed by her intellect and frank charm. A much told anecdote, in which she walks out of James's final exam after writing across the blue book, "Really I do not feel like an examination paper in philosophy today," lays claim to a precocious degree of self-possession. In fact, Stein felt sorely out of place in Cambridge. She was a Westerner with a European glaze among prim New Englanders. Her college essays—first-person confessionals steeped in romanticism—are artifacts of struggle. The grammar is shaky, and kernels of her nature prose, "The eternal feminine is nice to be sure but its painfully illogical," seem less a matter of intent than of verbal inadequacy. The essays portray anxious, strong-willed young women uncertain and frightened of their sexuality. Earnestly melodramatic, replete with hints of incest and sadomasochism, these characterizations were an attempt to control the many selves and voices that had risen up in the years of quiet isolation. Writing, like her interest in psychology, became a means of sorting through the mind's many choruses.

On James's recommendation, she attended Johns Hopkins Medical School to prepare for a career as a psychologist. After four years of study she grew bored and failed to graduate. Instead, she joined Leo in Europe, eventually settling in Paris on the Rue de Fleurus. There she completed her first novel, *Things As They Are*, a Henry James–like analysis of the emotional entanglements among three well-educated women. Based on Stein's thwarted affair with a Baltimore woman, the novel marked her acceptance of her sexual identity and confirmed her vocation as an author. In 1906, while working on her second book, she met Alice Toklas. Upper-class, Jewish, and a San Franciscan, she was comfortingly familiar to Stein. Toklas became both lover and eternally approving audience, devoting herself to domestic details which included typing each day the pages Stein would produce in all-night writing sessions. The evenings were reserved for callers, the days for picture-buying and tramping about Montmartre. In her salon and in her intimate relations with painters like Matisse, and especially Picasso, a surer, more forthright but decidedly aloof personality emerged—the Gertrude Stein of legend. Although her atelier was common ground for the many pre-war artistic revels, Stein was too bourgeois to endorse their less than proper antics. Yet she drew selectively on the ideas she heard debated nightly. Not a ringmaster but a cryptically wry observer, she preferred a crossroad to a cabal.

After the first world war, Rue de Fleurus became a shrine. It spread Stein's name around the world. Her public persona was clearly the product of deliberate design; she craved fame. Perhaps because of her solitary vantage and abiding sense of aloneness, she greatly desired acceptance; perhaps her experiments and the rejection she risked compelled her to declare her own genius. In any event, the decades following the war were dedicated to self-promotion, which culminated in the charming but nakedly egotistical *Autobiography of Alice B. Toklas*. Much like her friend and onetime student Hemingway, Stein labored hard at her myth, bringing forth an outsized creature that ranged beyond her control. As caricatures and jokes turned up in movies, comic strips, and musicals, the Bohemian *doyenne* superseded the author. She delighted in the celebrity, yet even within the ample confines of her fame she remained an island. Although she had served as midwife to the new century—studying psychology with James, abstract art with Picasso—Stein retained her roots in the 19th century. Distant and overwhelmed by propriety, part of her would not respond to the demands of modern fame. When *Four Saints in Three Acts* premiered in New York in 1934, her name was in lights on Broadway; she declined to attend and instead sent a note: "I rarely believe in anything because at the time of believing I am not really there to believe." Stein would hold fast to her apartness, a wise child among foreign tongues.

Thinking, for Stein, was not merely a prelude to composition but both its subject and method. In *Three Lives* she explored this notion. Especially in the "Melanctha" section, she created characters whose substance derived from an exacting transcription of their consciousness. They came to life in prose that circled at great remove from a barebones narrative, touching down only to jog it forward, then flying off. Published in 1909, the novel, her second, decisively announced her uniqueness. There was little precedent for *Three Lives*'s fidelity to the workings of human psychology. Only Henry James, at about the same time, pursued a similar goal. James took pleasure in the mind's propensity for hairsplitting refinements; he traced the balancing act in card-house sentences, sliding clause upon sub-clause. The elegance of his deftly constructed syntax suggests he may have conceived of the mind as an instrument powered by light and air to produce the music of a tuning fork's hum. Stein heard a rougher noise. Throughout *Three Lives* the rendering of the thinking mind suggests machinery hard at the task, clanking and catching, relentless. Her use of working-class and black-American dialects acquainted her with the expressive power of staggered rhythm and repetition. From these she fashioned a true sound, something closer to the core of consciousness.

Having recently arrived in Paris when she started *Three Lives*, Stein found her inspiration in Flaubert and Cézanne. Both were foremost among brother Leo's obsessions at the time. She worked at a translation of Flaubert's *Trois Contes* and absorbed the broad outline of the character Félicité from the story "*Un Coeur Simple.*" Félicité, a dying woman who has suffered quietly through a life of service to others, reminded Stein of the immigrant and black housekeepers and midwives she had known as a medical student in Baltimore. In their bruised, emotionally cramped lives she found a reflection of her own sexual and creative frustration. From Cézanne's paintings she took instruction in a method of depiction. Those paintings emphasized presence, the palpability of a face or vase. She wished to invest her trio of women—Anna, Lena, and Melanctha—with the undeniable reality of Cézanne's washwomen and cardplayers. She disdained biographical details and narrative plot and assembled her women in the "continuous present." In this newly created tense, "there was a constant recurring and beginning there was a marked direction of being in the present. . . ."

The characters manifest themselves at every point in the telling as a painting offers its subject completely from any particular view. Verbal tics like Melanctha's tireless repetition of the word "certainly" serve as apertures through which she is apprehended whole. Thus the speaker's rhythms become indistinguishable from the speaker; in fact, they express an essence: "Melanctha Herbert was always losing what she had in wanting all the things she saw. Melanctha was always being left when she was not leaving others. Melanctha Herbert always loved too hard and much too often." Stein used language as an impressionist painter used color, to catch what William James called the "vague and inarticulate" dimension of conscious life. This is not the artful stream of consciousness of Joyce. In the ebb and flow of Melanctha's thought, there is a music unique and quotidian as a signature; Stein wrote the mind the way she heard it.

If, as Stein proclaimed, *Three Lives* was literature's first step into the new century, *The Making of Americans* may find a home in the next. Intractable, interminable, yet strangely mesmerizing, the novel resides in the black hole of literary history. In the 75 years since its completion, *Americans* has been in print only sporadically, most often in abridged editions. Rarely seen, more rarely read, its 925 densely printed pages offer some of the knottiest prose in the language. Few have the stamina (myself included) to plow from cover to cover. Lacking any formal organization, narrative logic, or even a place to rest, the writing proceeds at full pitch, battering through the notion of the well-made novel. Stein believed *Americans* to be her masterpiece. She regarded it with great affection and kept faith with its most egregious flaws. When she proofed the galleys, few changes were made: "I always found myself forced back into its incorrectness." She knew those flaws—the bottomless sentences, badly joined narrative, and ragged pacing—constituted the voice she had struggled to achieve. Writing at a time of emotional isolation, she battled the deep suspicion that her unorthodox method was consigned to failure. She both doubted and wished to embrace her "incorrectness": "I have been very glad to have been wrong. It is sometimes a very hard thing to win myself to having been wrong about something. I do a great deal of suffering." The admissions of uncertainty recur throughout *Americans*. Her "big book," as she called it, was very much about the making of Gertrude Stein. It served as the laboratory of her own self-discovery, in which she sought the "great author inside one."

The quest for greatness explains the immense sprawl. *Americans* is overcrowded by Stein's many ambitions. With Olympian naiveté, she said her intent was to "describe really describe every kind of human being that ever was or is or would be." She also wanted to indulge an autobiographical impulse and tell the story of her German-Jewish immigrant family, then draw from their experience—"the old people in a new world, the new people made out of the old"—a transcendent national archetype. Even the novel would take on a representative function as "an essentially American book." Stein plunged ahead on all fronts but failed to keep step. Her rich ideation outraced her ability to shape a coherently multidimensional fiction. The same unvaried single-mindedness that flexed strangely in her prose made for a crude reductionism in the realm of conception. Preferring stark opposition to shading and ambiguity, Stein lacked the intellectual cast to balance the conflicting demands of so many goals. In the end, mythmaking and family history run poor seconds to the psychologist's urge to describe and classify.

Americans's fictional family, the Herslands, are recognizable as the Steins, and their daughter Martha as the author, yet there is little of the specificity of detail we expect from an autobiographical novel. Relations between characters are broadly sketched and narrative development is bound by the continuous present; everyone is in a state of becoming. The extensive use of pronouns—he, she, one, some, they—helps contain the characters' reality within the scope of clinical report. The flatness is deliberate; the characters appear like many different masks behind which Stein makes the case that everyone is different but the same. The Herslands sit in as typological specimens for an extended meditation on behavioral patterns and patterns of description: "There are many ways of making kinds of men and women. In each way of making kinds of them there is a different system of finding them resembling. Sometime there will be here every way there can be of seeing kinds of men and women." As in *Three Lives*, the rhythms of speech embody what Stein termed a character's "bottom nature." "Slowly, more and more, one gets to know them as repeating comes out in them. In the middle of their living they are always repeating. . . ." However, the novel is less about "kinds," "ones," and Americans than it is about the mind obsessed with these distinctions. *The Making of Americans* is a driven book, as relentless as many of its dithyrambic, train-length sentences. Stein set herself the task of thinking on paper for a thousand pages until she had "not many things but one thing." What she had was an artifact of consciousness, a mind's true life played out as the "steady pound of repeating."

Americans liberated Stein from tentativeness and self-doubt and confirmed her break from any fealty to conventional structure or syntax. She had pushed past telling into a new arrangement with the reader, one in which the reader felt the text become itself. In *Tender Buttons* and her portraits, she pushed even further. Struck by the composition of Picasso's cubist collages, she noted that "to have brought the objects together already changed them to other things, not to another picture but to something else, to things as Picasso saw them." In her middle, or *Tender Buttons*, period, Stein pursued the same effect. Like the Cubists, she would avoid literal representation in depicting objects and people. She found a compositional equivalent to cubist recombination in "the ridding myself of nouns." *Tender Buttons* describes things without mentioning them, without metaphoric comparison. Instead, Stein adopted the cubist approach of looking at an object from many perspectives, then collapsing the impressions into a single expressive image:

CARELESS WATER
No cup is broken in more places and mended, that is to say a plate is broken and mending does do that it shows that culture is Japanese. It shows the whole element of angels and orders. It does more to choosing and it does more to that ministering counting. It dies, it does change in more water.

Although *Tender Buttons* was written in 1911, the boldness of the experiment remains unmuted. We have grown accustomed enough to cubist and abstract visuals that they can be used in advertisements, but a line like "The change in that is that red weakens an hour" still unsettles us. Yet these prose poems were not meant to shock; they were launched from familiar ground. Stein chose household items—*A Carafe, A Red Hat,* or *A Seltzer Bottle*—along with abstract but homey commonplaces like *In Between, A Time to Eat,* and *A Centre in a Table.* To each she responded with a subjectivity so unyielding that the relationship between text and object is indecipherable. *Malachite*: "The sudden spoon is the same in no size. The sudden spoon is the wound in the decision." *Cold Climate* abstracts abstraction: "A Season in yellow sold extra strings makes lying places." What is a "lying place"? The usage and grammar are still so fresh we have the impression we are reading a distorted translation from another language, or maybe the ramblings of an aphasiac. The logic of the connections, whether hallucinatory or mundane, is rigorously private. Stein rendered interpretation futile; she preferred her reader to enter the synesthetic domain of the poem and respond as subjectively as the author had.

"Language as a real thing," Stein wrote in "Poetry and Grammar," "is not imitation either of sounds or colors or emotions it is an intellectual recreation. . . ." In *Toklas* she credits her work with "the destruction of the associational emotion in poetry and prose." She was adamant about disconnecting texts from predictable reactions. She believed in the use of language as an end in itself, not as a medium of expression but as a vital expressive element. It's clear that language lacks the plasticity of color or a musical note. It is inescapably tied to a denotative intent. Stein chafed at this limit but recognized it; she simply wanted to lengthen the leash. By placing words in unworn sequences, the dislocated sentences in *Tender Buttons* restored substantiality, a thingness, to desiccated syllables. This was the thinking behind her notorious "rose is a rose is a rose." In that line, Stein remarked, "the rose is red for the first time in English poetry for a hundred years."

Her attraction to painting and its suggestive capacity also led to a series of word portraits in which she attempted to depict with "exactitude" her subject's "inner and outer reality." Usually made for close friends—Matisse, Picasso, Sherwood Anderson—the portraits continued exploring the relation between description and types: "In doing a portrait of any one, the repetition consists in knowing that that one is a kind of a one, that the things he does have been done by others like him that the things he says have been said by others like him. . . ." After having "talked and listened" to her subject, she recreated what struck her as essential. The *Portrait of Mabel Dodge*, written in 1911, introduced Stein's textual cubism to the literary world. Dodge was so flattered by the piece she had 300 copies reprinted and bound in Florentine wallpaper (an inspired stroke on her part) and distributed them to the New York literati, who were confused by "so much breathing has not the same place where there is that much beginning. . . . So much breathing has the same place and there must not be so much suggestion. There can be there the habit that there is if there is no need of resting. The absence is not alternative." Because it felt arbitrary it was deemed gibberish. Stein's composition relied less on randomness as a method than on creating the effect of randomness for the reader. No doubt, Stein rummaged freely in shaping her impressions, but her vocabulary was carefully circumscribed by the demands of each piece, and the internal rhythmic and imagistic consistency rarely wavered. She manipulated a sense of semantic chaos so that her reader might find new points of entry into old words or discover a delicious strangeness in an ordinary notion. Her "gibberish" slowed the eye and allowed the words to be pronounced on the tongue and in the ear.

The randomness irked many readers. In 1934 B. F. Skinner publicized experiments Stein had helped conduct at Harvard investigating the possibility of automatic writing. He charged that *Tender Buttons* was the product of just such a process, and his claim became a convenient reason for dismissing her work. Stein denied, in several contradictory statements, any connection, and her partisans have been at pains to echo her denials. The skill in Stein's wordplay and linguistic technique is too obvious to attribute to chance, but that doesn't preclude some role for the principles behind automatic writing. She wrote each day for a specific amount of time (occasionally sitting in her Ford while Toklas ran errands) and tended to revise very little. The immediacy she sought was diluted by revision and heightened by the need to fill the page. Stein's craftsmanship appears keener when its improvisatory component is understood; her incremental variations on a single phrase are closer in spirit to a musician like Charlie Parker than they are to any other writer.

In her poems and librettos, Stein openly aspired to the persistent music of lyric verse. The repetitions are carefully layered so they accumulate into melodic, rolling tones. Some phrases in *Four Saints in Three Acts* mimic tribal chant: "Saints settled saints settled all in all saints. All saints. Saints in all saints. Saint settlement." There is a litter of mantra-like bits of nonsense—"windows and windows and ones"—that infiltrate the mind to stay. The long poems—"Lifting Belly," "Patriarchal Poetry," and "Stanzas in Meditation"—thrive on swung measure and song. The availability of line breaks and verse's more open page encouraged Stein to parse out her compound run-on sentences, as if she needed the clutterless white expanse to keep track of their unpackaged parts. The line breaks in "Stanzas in Meditation" create breathing room the prose lacks and demonstrate just how she built sentences from clauses:

> *Full well I know that she is there*
> *Much as she will she can be there*
> *But which I know which I know when*
> *Which is my way to be there then*
> *Which she will know as I know here*
> *That it is now that it is there*

The metrics are as basic as the meaning is opaque. Typically, abstract words like "which," "when," and "there" have been placed to connote some tangible representation, teasing our expectation that the poem might refer to a reality outside itself. For Stein the text can be an autonomous thing, its references bound within its actual occurrence, within the continuous present. Meaning isn't a matter of referring but rather of becoming. In contrast, "Lifting Belly," an erotic hymn to Toklas, is rich in specific details about their daily life together:

> *Can you can you*
> *Can you buy a Ford*
> *Did you expect that*
> *Lifting belly hungrily*

> *Not lonesomely*
> *But enthusiastically*
> *Lifting belly altogether*
> *Were you wise*
> *Were you wise to do so.*

The coy bits of personal trivia—what car Stein owned—don't require exegesis; a better clue to their intimate lives might be found in the poem's odd mix of nursery-rhyme singsong and the language of passion. Regardless of whether her writing skirts second- and third-tier abstraction or turns on a sexual pun, Stein's subject is always herself. By purging language of its stock associations, she claimed she could invest words with a new reality. In fact, what she did was shape a language that is wholly her own. At a time when many writers pressed to expand the self to include a world, Stein drew the world in upon herself. She devised a system of relations, a grammar of reference, that posited her at its center.

During her lifetime, Stein served as her own best critic. The job was not sought by many. Her writing was too extraordinary to attract a ready crew of village explainers. Having stirred so much curiosity about her life and work, she took to explicating herself. And she enjoyed the work. The strong element of public performance in her essays (even those she never delivered as lectures) indicates she relished the opportunity to instruct. An invitation to speak at Oxford in 1926 provided the occasion for her first critical essay. Appearing before a standing-room audience, she treated them to the uncompromisingly knotty "Composition as Explanation." What the dons made of roundabout dictates like "Romanticism is then when everything being alike everything is naturally simply different" is anyone's guess. She did make clear that her difficult style was not a clever conceit to be put off when it was time to talk shop. Her method of exploring characters in fictions should be as useful and legitimate for explaining that method in an essay. She insisted her writing be of one piece. For example, the assembling and dissembling paragraphs and sentences in *How To Write* discuss her techniques while employing them. Consequently, when she talks about specific works, it becomes unclear where the fiction leaves off and the explanation begins. "The Gradual Making of the Making of Americans," a blueprint made in retrospect, could blend imperceptibly into the novel.

The closed circuit of the critical exchange—Stein analyzing Stein—suggests an unabashed solipsism, which she most enthusiastically practiced. But it also gives some measure of her originality and its isolating effect. She could cite no literary forebears for her mature style, and comparisons with contemporaries were limited to those whom she'd influenced. Stein built, occupied, and still dwells in a room truly of her own. Her early publications were self-subsidized; she was 59 and had been writing for over 30 years when an American publisher finally accepted a book of hers; much of her writing was published posthumously, some not at all; today her presence in American bookstores and universities is sporadic, always qualified. It is ironic that a writer whose aesthetic enterprise was so tied to the reader and the experience of reading should find an audience hard to come by.

Nevertheless, she is without doubt one of the most influential writers of the century. Her list of debtors, direct and indirect, is uncountably long. Sherwood Anderson proudly acknowledged the impact of *Three Lives*. Hemingway, who typed sizable portions of *Americans*, was less candid, but his bluntly clipped sentences and notions of suggestive detail are obviously Stein's. ("The worst, he said, were the women with dead babies. You couldn't get the women to give up their dead babies. They'd have babies dead for six days. Wouldn't give them up.") Her stark rhythms and repetitions were absorbed by writers as diverse as Beckett and Chandler, the "steady pound of repeating" embodied this century's rebellion against the florid arabesques of the Victorian era. Like Picasso's recovery of the primitive eye through his use of masks, Stein restored to language its connection to the spoken. Her demolition of grammatical constraint stirred almost every American author and practically spawned a homegrown (not European inspired) tradition of experimental writing. She proved that sentences needn't stop when the rules said so, but could roll on till they exhausted themselves. Faulkner and Kerouac took note. Her painterly approach, the power she sprang from the performance of words as words launched the Language poets, one of the most vital movements in postwar American writing. In a broader sense, the example of her life, her Yankee stubbornness and subversive vigor, cut the cloth for the American avant garde style in all the arts. Indeed, she is the mother of us all.

"Think of anything," Stein wrote, "of cowboys, of movies, of detective stories, of anybody who does anywhere or stays at home and is an American and you will realize that it is something strictly American to conceive a space that is filled with moving, a space of time that is filled always filled with moving. . . ." She brought the continuous movement of the mind, with its churned and unresting music, to the page. She conjured an immediacy that made reading new. "I am writing for myself and strangers," she announced in *The Making of Americans*. Yet she brings those strangers close to the act of written creation, so close inside her struggle with the sayable that we cannot remain strangers very long. To read Stein is to relinquish our place outside the text and to begin with her to make the words make sense.

Chronology

1864	Gertrude Stein's parents, Amelia (Keyser) Stein (b. 1842) and Daniel Stein (b. 1832), marry.
1865	Their son Michael is born.
1867	Their second son, Simon, is born.
1870	Their daughter Bertha is born.
1872	Their third son, Leo, is born.
1874	3 February, Gertrude Stein born in Allegheny, Pennsylvania.
1875–1878	Stein family makes its residence variously in Austria and France.
1877	30 April, Alice B. Toklas born in San Francisco, California.
1879	Stein family moves to Baltimore, Maryland.
1880	Stein family moves to Oakland, California.
1885	Amelia Stein becomes ill with cancer.
1888	Stein attends Oakland High School. Amelia Stein dies.
1891	Daniel Stein dies. Remaining family members stay together, headed by oldest brother Michael.
1892	Stein goes to live with a maternal aunt in Baltimore. Brother Leo leaves for study at University of California, Berkeley.
1893	After an uneven primary and secondary education, Stein follows Leo to Harvard and as a special student without a high school diploma enters Harvard Annex (later renamed Radcliffe). While there, she studies with William James.
1894	Conducts laboratory work for psychologist Hugo Münsterberg.

1896   Publishes "Normal Motor Automatism," with Leon Solomons, in Harvard's *Psychological Review.*

1897   Leaves Harvard Annex, having been refused her degree after failing a Latin examination.

1897–1901   Enters Johns Hopkins Medical School, where Leo is studying biology, and studies medicine for four years.

1898   Receives her undergraduate degree. Publishes a second article, "Cultivated Motor Automatism," in the *Psychological Review.*

1901   Fails four courses in her final term of medical school and so earns no advanced degree.

1902   Moves to London with Leo. Later that year, Leo moves to Paris.

1903   Moves to Paris, again accompanying Leo, and resides with him until 1912. Spends winter in New York with friends, including Mabel Weeks.

1904   Commences in earnest collecting paintings with Leo. Visits the United States for the last time until her lecture tour.

1905   Meets artist Pablo Picasso. Salon at 27 Rue de Fleurus begins.

1907   Toklas and Stein meet in Paris. Stein poses for Picasso's portrait of her.

1908   Toklas begins to participate in Stein's writing career by learning to type and transcribing manuscripts.

1909   Toklas takes up residence at Stein's home, 27 Rue de Fleurus. First book, *Three Lives,* published. Begins work on "A Long Gay Book" (completed 1912).

1910   Begins work on "Many Many Women" (completed 1912).

1911   Starts writing *G.M.P.* (completed 1912). Completes *The Making of Americans.*

1912   Alfred Stieglitz publishes Stein's portraits, "Matisse" and "Picasso," in *Camera Work.*

1913   Leo moves out of 27 Rue de Fleurus, decisively marking a break in his previous relationship with his sister.

1914   *Tender Buttons* published. War begins.

1915   Stein and Toklas go to Spain, where Stein enjoys watching bullfights.

1916   Stein and Toklas return to Paris.

1917   Writes "Lifting Belly." Drives supply van ("Auntie") for American Fund for French Wounded, World War I.

1919   Stein and Toklas return to Paris.

1920   Purchases "Godiva," the automobile featured in several of her writings.

1921   Writes "A Sonatina Followed by Another." Meets writer Sherwood Anderson. Lipchitz creates bronze head of Gertrude Stein. Leo marries Nina Auzias.

1922   Composes "Didn't Nelly and Lilly Love You," "American Biography and Why Waste It," and "A Singular Addition." *Geography and Plays* published. Meets writer Ernest Hemingway and artist Man Ray.

1923   Writes "Subject-Cases: The Background of a Detective Story," "A Book," "As A Wife Has A Cow A Love Story," and "An Instant Answer or a Hundred Prominent Men."

1924   Writes "Birth and Marriage." Portions of *The Making of Americans* appear in *transatlantic review*.

1925   *The Making of Americans* (1906–1911) published as book.

1926   "Composition as Explanation" given as talk at Cambridge and Oxford, also published with the same title. Meets composer Virgil Thomson and Bernard Faÿ. Spends time at Hotel Pernollet, where events occur that inspire her detective story, *Blood on the Dining-Room Floor*.

1927   Writes "Patriarchal Poetry." Begins to wear her "Caesar" haircut.

1928   Writes "A Lyrical Opera Made By Two To Be Sung." *Useful Knowledge* published.

1929   Stein and Toklas lease house at Bilignin.

1930   Writes "We Came a History." Meets James Joyce at Jo Davidson's studio, and meets Francis Rose.

1931   *Lucy Church Amiably* and *How To Write* published.

1932   Writes *Autobiography of Alice B. Toklas* at Bilignin. Publishes *Operas and Plays* and *How to Write*.

1933   *Autobiography of Alice B. Toklas* and *G.M.P.* published. Madame Pernollet dies in a fall. Writes *Blood on the Dining-Room Floor* and "Four in America." *Autobiography* becomes a bestseller.

1934   8 February, *Four Saints in Three Acts* debuts in Hartford, Connecticut, New York City, and Chicago. Stein and Toklas arrive in the United States on 24 October. Begins to deliver her "Lectures in America," published in 1935 under that title. 12 November, conducts radio interview with William Lundell. 27 November, Stein and Toklas ride along with homicide police. *Poems and Prayers* published.

1935   30 January, records readings aloud. February, publication of "Testimony Against Gertrude Stein," by *transition*. 1 April, party at home of Lillian May Ehrman acquaints Stein with Charlie Chaplin, Dashiell Hammett, Lillian Hellman, Paulette Goddard, and Anita Loos. Lecture tour continues. Stein and Toklas return to France on 4 May. Writes *Narration,* "American Crimes and How They Matter," "American Newspapers," "I Came and Here I Am" "What Are Masterpieces," and "How Writing Is Written."

1936   Lectures at Oxford and Cambridge. *Geographical History of America* published. Writes *Everybody's Autobiography*.

1937   Writes "Why I Like Detective Stories." Publishes *Everybody's Autobiography*. Attends London premiere of *A Wedding Bouquet* (ballet). Meets Thornton Wilder.

1938   Stein and Toklas move to 5 rue Christine.

1939   Stein writes and publishes *The World Is Round*. Because of the war, Stein and Toklas close Paris apartment and move to Bilignin. Writes "My Debt to Books."

1940   Germany occupies Paris. Writes *Alphabets and Birthdays*. Publishes *What Are Masterpieces?*

1943   Stein and Toklas move to Culoz.

1944   Stein and Toklas return to Paris in December.

1945   Lectures in Brussels. Tours American army bases in occupied Germany.

1946   Writes "Reflections on the Atomic Bomb." *Yes Is For a Very Young Man* debuts in Pasadena. Is ill with cancer in Neuilly-sur-Seire, dies on 27 July, and is buried in Pere Lachaise Cemetery, Paris. *Selected Writings of Gertrude Stein* published.

1947   Leo Stein dies.

1967   Alice B. Toklas dies.

Selected Bibliography

Primary Sources

Manuscripts

Gertrude Stein Papers. The Yale Collection of American Literature. Beinecke Rare Book and Manuscript Library. Yale University, New Haven, Conn.

Publications

Books

Three Lives. New York: Vintage Books, 1909.

Tender Buttons. New York: Haskell House, 1914.

Geography and Plays. Boston: Four Seas, 1922.

Composition As Explanation. Garden City, N.Y.: Doubleday, 1928.

Useful Knowledge. New York: Payson and Clarke, 1928.

Lucy Church Amiably. Paris: Imprimerie Union, 1930.

How to Write. Paris: Plain Edition, 1931.

Operas and Plays. Paris: Plain Edition, 1932.

The Autobiography of Alice B. Toklas. New York: Vintage Books, 1933.

Four Saints in Three Acts. New York: Modern Library, 1934.

The Making of Americans: The Hersland Family. New York: Harcourt, Brace, 1934.

Portraits and Prayers. New York: Random House, 1934.

Lectures in America. New York: Random House, 1935.

Narration: Four Lectures by Gertrude Stein. Introduction by Thornton Wilder. Chicago: University of Chicago Press, 1935.

The Geographical History of America or The Relation of Human Nature to the Human Mind. Introduction by Thornton Wilder. New York: Random House, 1936.

What Are Masterpieces? Ed. Robert Bartlett Haas. Los Angeles: Black Sparrow, 1940.

The Gertrude Stein First Reader and Three Plays. Dublin: M. Friedberg, 1946.

Selected Writings of Gertrude Stein. Ed. Carl Van Vechten. New York: Vintage Books, 1946.

Four in America. Introduction by Thornton Wilder. New Haven, Conn.: Yale University Press, 1947.

Blood on the Dining-Room Floor. Foreword by Donald Gallup. Pawlet, Vt.: Banyon, 1948.

Last Operas and Plays. Ed. Carl Van Vechten. New York: Rinehart, 1949.

Things as They Are: A Novel in Three Parts. Pawlet, Vt.: Banyan, 1950.

Two: Gertrude Stein and Her Brother and Other Early Portraits. Foreword by Janet Flanner. New Haven, Conn.: Yale University Press, 1951.

Mrs. Reynolds and Five Earlier Novelettes. Foreword by Lloyd Frankenberg. New Haven, Conn.: Yale University Press, 1952.

As Fine as Melanctha. Foreword by Natalie Clifford Barney. New Haven, Conn.: Yale University Press, 1953.

Bee Time Vine and Other Pieces. Freeport, Maine: Books for Libraries, 1953.

Painted Lace and Other Pieces. Introduction by Daniel-Henry Kahnweiler. New Haven, Conn.: Yale University Press, 1955.

Stanzas in Meditation and Other Poems. New Haven, Conn.: Yale University Press, 1956.

Alphabets and Birthdays. Introduction by Donald Gallup. Freeport, Maine: Books for Libraries, 1957.

A Novel of Thank You. Introduction by Carl Van Vechten. New Haven, Conn.: Yale University Press, 1958.

Gertrude Stein's America. Ed. Gilbert Harrison. Washington, D.C.: Luce, 1965.

Gertrude Stein: Writings and Lectures, 1911–1945. Ed. Patricia Meyerowitz. London: Peter Owen, 1967.

Gertrude Stein on Picasso. Ed. Edward Burns. New York: Liveright, 1970.

Selected Operas and Plays of Gertrude Stein. Ed. John Malcolm Brinnen. Pittsburgh, Pa.: University of Pittsburgh Press, 1970.

Everybody's Autobiography. New York: Cooper Square Publishers, 1971.

"Fernhurst," "Q.E.D.," and Other Early Writings. Ed. Leon Katz. New York: Liveright, 1971.

Matisse Picasso and Gertrude Stein with Two Shorter Stories. Boston: Something Else, 1972.

How Writing Is Written. Ed. Robert Bartlett Haas. Los Angeles: Black Sparrow, 1974.

Reflections on the Atomic Bomb. Los Angeles: Black Sparrow, 1974.

The World Is Round. San Francisco: North Point, 1988.

Lifting Belly. Ed. Rebecca Mark. Tallahassee: NAIAD, 1989.

Gertrude Stein: Writings 1903–1932. Ed. Catharine Stimpson and Harriet Chessman. New York: Library of America, 1998.

Gertrude Stein: Writings 1932–1946. Ed. Catharine Stimpson and Harriet Chessman. New York: Library of America, 1998.

Articles

"Cultivated Motor Automatism: A Study of Character in Its Relation to Attention." *The Psychological Review* 3 (May 1898): 295–306.

"And now; And so the time comes when I can tell the story of my life." *Vanity Fair,* September 1934, 35, 65.

Interviews

"Gertrude Stein: A Radio Interview." Interview by William Lundell. WJZ and NET, 12 November 1934. Typescript. Gertrude Stein Papers. The Yale Collection of American Literature. Beinecke Rare Book and Manuscript Library. Yale University, New Haven, Conn.

"The Situation in American Writing." *Partisan Review* 6, no. 4 (1939), 24–51.

Correspondence

Burns, Edward, ed. *Staying on Alone: Letters of Alice B. Toklas.* Garden City, N.Y.: Liveright, 1973.

————, ed. *The Letters of Gertrude Stein and Carl Van Vechten.* New York: Columbia University Press, 1986.

Burns, Edward, and Ulla E. Dydo, eds., with the assistance of William Rice. *The Letters of Gertrude Stein and Thornton Wilder.* New Haven, Conn.: Yale University Press, 1996.

Steward, Samuel, ed. *Dear Sammy: Letters from Gertrude Stein.* Boston: Houghton Mifflin, 1977.

Secondary Sources

Critical Studies: Books and Dissertations

Andrews, Bruce, and Charles Bernstein, eds. *The L=A=N=G=U=A=G=E Book.* Carbondale: Southern Illinois University Press, 1984.

Benstock, Shari. *Women of the Left Bank.* Austin: University of Texas Press, 1986.

Berry, Ellen. *Curved Thought and Textual Wandering: Gertrude Stein's Postmodernism.* Ann Arbor: University of Michigan Press, 1992.

Bloom, Harold, ed. *Gertrude Stein: Modern Critical Views.* New Haven, Conn.: Chelsea House, 1986.

Bowers, Jane Palatini. *Gertrude Stein.* New York: St. Martin's, 1992.

Bridgman, Richard. *Gertrude Stein in Pieces.* New York: Oxford University Press, 1970.

Brinnen, John. *The Third Rose: Gertrude Stein and Her World.* Boston: Little, Brown, 1959.

Bush, Clive. *Halfway to Revolution: Investigation and Crisis in the Work of Henry Adams, William James, and Gertrude Stein.* New Haven, Conn.: Yale University Press, 1991.

Caramello, Charles. *Henry James, Gertrude Stein, and the Biographical Act.* Chapel Hill: University of North Carolina Press, 1996.

Cerf, Bennett. *Try and Stop Me.* New York: Simon and Schuster, 1944.

Chessman, Harriet. *The Public Is Invited to Dance: Representation, the Body, and Dialogue in Gertrude Stein.* Stanford, Calif.: Stanford University Press, 1989.

Dearborn, Mary. *Pocohontas's Daughters: Gender and Ethnicity in American Culture.* New York: Oxford University Press, 1986.

DeKoven, Marianne. *A Different Language: Gertrude Stein's Experimental Writing.* Madison: University of Wisconsin Press, 1983.

———. *Rich and Strange: Gender, History, Modernism.* Princeton: Princeton University Press, 1991.

Dickie, Margaret. *Stein, Bishop, and Rich: Lyrics of Love, War, and Place.* Chapel Hill: University of North Carolina Press, 1997.

Doane, Janice. *Silence and Narrative: The Early Novels of Gertrude Stein.* Westport, Conn.: Greenwood, 1986.

Douglas, Ann. *Terrible Honesty: Mongrel Manhattan in the 1920s.* New York: Farrar, Straus, and Giroux, 1995.

Dydo, Ulla E., ed. *A Stein Reader.* Evanston, Ill.: Northwestern University Press, 1993.

Fifer, Elizabeth. *Rescued Readings: A Reconstruction of Gertrude Stein's Difficult Texts.* Detroit, Mich.: Wayne State University Press, 1992.

Fleischmann, Fritz, ed. *American Novelists Revisited: Essays in Feminist Criticism.* New York: G. K. Hall, 1982.

Foreman, Richard. *Plays and Manifestos.* New York: New York University Press, 1976.

Garvin, Harry. "Gertrude Stein: A Study of Her Theory and Practice." Ph.D. diss., University of Michigan, 1950.

Grahn, Judy. *Another Mother Tongue: Gay Words, Gay Worlds.* Boston: Beacon, 1984.

———. *The Highest Apple: Sappho and the Lesbian Poetic Tradition.* San Francisco: Spinsters, Ink, 1985.

———. *Really Reading Gertrude Stein: A Selected Anthology.* Freedom, Calif.: Crossing Press, 1989.

Haas, Robert Bartlett. *A Primer for the Gradual Understanding of Gertrude Stein.* Los Angeles: Black Sparrow, 1971.

Hartley, George. *Textual Politics and the Language Poets.* Bloomington: Indiana University Press, 1989.

Hoffman, Frederick. *Gertrude Stein.* Minneapolis: University of Minnesota Press, 1961.

Hoffman, Michael. *The Development of Abstractionism in the Writings of Gertrude Stein.* Philadelphia: University of Pennsylvania Press, 1965.

———. *Gertrude Stein.* Boston: Twayne, 1976.

———. *Critical Essays on Gertrude Stein.* Boston: G. K. Hall, 1986.

Hurd, Edith Thacher. *The World Is Not Flat: A Square Companion Volume to the Round Edition of "The World Is Round," Containing the Publishing History of Gertrude Stein's Book for Children (and Adults).* New York: Arion, n.d.

Selected Bibliography

Jones, Lilla Maria Crisafulli, and Vita Fortunati, eds. *Rittratto dell'artista come donna: Saggi sull'avanguardia del Novecento*. Urbino, Italy: QuattroVenti, 1988.

Jurak, Mirko, ed. *Cross-Cultural Studies: American, Canadian, and European Literatures: 1945–1985*. Ljubljana, Yugoslavia: Filozofska Fakulteta, 1988.

Katz, Leon. "The First Making of *The Making of Americans*: A Study Based on Gertrude Stein's Notebooks and Early Version of Her Novel." Ph.D. diss., Columbia University, 1963.

Kellner, Bruce. *A Gertrude Stein Companion: Content with the Example*. Westport, N.Y.: Greenwood, 1988.

Knapp, Bettina. *Gertrude Stein*. New York: Continuum, 1990.

Kostelanetz, Richard, ed. *The Yale Gertrude Stein*. New Haven, Conn.: Yale University Press, 1980.

————, ed. *Gertrude Stein Advanced: An Anthology of Criticism*. Jefferson, N.C.: McFarland, 1990.

Meese, Elizabeth A., *(Ex)Tensions: Re-Figuring Feminist Criticism*. Chicago: University of Chicago Press, 1990.

————. *(Sem)erotics: Theorizing Lesbian:Writing*. New York: New York University Press, 1992.

Middlebrook, Diane, and Marilyn Yalom, eds. *Coming to Light: American Women Poets in the Twentieth Century*. Ann Arbor: University of Michigan Press, 1985.

Miller, Rosalind. *Gertrude Stein: Form and Intelligibility, Containing the Radcliffe Themes Edited from the Manuscripts in the Yale University Library*. New York: Exposition, 1949.

Neuman, Shirley, and Ira Nadel, eds. *Gertrude Stein and the Making of Literature*. Boston: Northeastern University Press, 1988.

Orenstein, Gloria. *The Reflowering of the Goddess: Contemporary Journeys and Cycles of Empowerment*. New York: Pergamon, 1990.

Perelman, Robert. *The Trouble with Genius: Reading Pound, Joyce, Stein, and Zukofsky*. Berkeley: University of California Press, 1994.

Perloff, Marjorie. *Poetic License: Essays on Modernist and Postmodernist Lyric*. Evanston, Ill.: Northwestern University Press, 1990.

Perry, Ruth, and Marine Watson Brownley, eds. *Mothering the Mind: Twelve Studies of Writers and Their Silent Partners*. New York: Holmes and Meier, 1984.

Rieke, Alison. *The Senses of Nonsense*. Iowa City: University of Iowa Press, 1992.

Rogers, W. G. *Gertrude Stein Is Gertrude Stein Is Gertrude Stein: Her Life and Work*. New York: Crowell, 1973.

Ruddick, Lisa. *Reading Gertrude Stein: Body, Text, Gnosis*. Ithaca, N.Y.: Cornell University Press, 1990.

Ryan, Betsy Alayne. *Gertrude Stein's Theatre of the Absolute*. Ann Arbor: University Microfilms International, 1984.

Scott, Bonnie. *The Gender of Modernism: A Critical Anthology*. Bloomington: Indiana University Press, 1990.

Simon, Linda, ed. *Gertrude Stein: A Composite Portrait*. New York: Avon Books, 1974.

————, ed. *Gertrude Stein Remembered*. Lincoln: University of Nebraska Press, 1994.

Sprigge, Elizabeth. *Gertrude Stein: Her Life and Work*. New York: Harper and Brothers, 1957.

Steiner, Wendy. *Exact Resemblance to Exact Resemblance: The Literary Portraiture of Gertrude Stein*. New Haven, Conn.: Yale University Press, 1978.

Stendhal, Renate, ed. *Gertrude Stein: In Words and Pictures; A Photobiography*. Chapel Hill, N.C.: Algonquin, 1994.

Stewart, Allegra. *Gertrude Stein and the Present*. Cambridge, Mass.: Harvard University Press, 1967.

Suleiman, Susan, ed. *The Female Body in Western Civilization: Contemporary Perspectives*. Cambridge, Mass.: Harvard University Press, 1986.

Sutherland, Donald. *Gertrude Stein: A Biography of Her Work*. New Haven, Conn.: Yale University Press, 1951.

Thomas, F. Richard. *Literary Admirers of Alfred Stieglitz*. Carbondale: Southern Illinois University Press, 1951.

Toklas, Alice B. *What is Remembered*. New York: Holt, Rinehart, and Winston, 1963.

Van Vechten, Carl. *Fragments from an Unwritten Autobiography*. New Haven, Conn.: Yale University Library, 1955.

Walker, Jayne. *The Making of a Modernist: Gertrude Stein from 'Three Lives' to 'Tender Buttons.'* Amherst: University of Massachusetts Press, 1984.

Warner, Elinor Hope. " 'Officer, She's Writing Again': Gertrude Stein's American Readers." Ph.D. diss., University of Virginia, 1994.

Watts, Linda. *Rapture Untold: Gender, Mysticism, and 'The Moment of Recognition' in the Writings of Gertrude Stein*. New York: Lang, 1996.

Weinstein, Norman. *Gertrude Stein and the Literature of the Modern Consciousness*. New York: Frederick Ungar, 1970.

Welch, Lew. *How I Read Gertrude Stein*. San Francisco: Grey Fox, 1996.

Wilson, Edmund. *Axel's Castle: A Study in the Imaginative Literature of 1870–1930*. New York: Scribner's, 1931.

Critical Works: Articles and Book Chapters

Agee, James. "Stein's Way." *Time*, 11 September 1933, 57–60.

Baker, William. "Stein Put Down Hecklers after University Lecture." *Lost Generation Journal* 4, no. 1 (1976): 24, 31.

Benstock, Shari. "Paris, Lesbianism, and the Politics of Reaction, 1900–1940." In *Hidden From History: Reclaiming the Gay and Lesbian Past*, ed. Martin Bauml Duberman, Martha Vicinus, and George Chauncey Jr. New York: New American Library, 1989.

Berry, Ellen. "On Reading Gertrude Stein." *Genders* 5 (Summer 1989): 1–20.

————. "Gertrude Stein's Utopian Dialogics." *Contemporary Literature* 30, no. 4 (1989): 573–77.

Chessman, Harriet. "Representation and the Female: Gertrude Stein's 'Lifting Belly' and *Tender Buttons.*" In *The Book of the Self: Person, Pretext, and Process,* ed. Polly Young-Eisendrath and James A. Hall. New York: New York University Press, 1987.

Cook, Blanche Wiesen. " 'Women Alone Stir My Imagination': Lesbianism and the Cultural Tradition." *Signs* 4, no. 4 (1979): 718–39.

Cope, Karin. "Painting after Gertrude Stein." *Diacritics* 24, no. 2–3 (1994): 190–203.

Davidson, Michael. "On Reading Gertrude Stein," In *The L=A=N=G=U=A=G=E Book,* ed. Bruce Andrews and Charles Bernstein. Carbondale: Southern Illinois University Press, 1984.

DeKoven, Marianne. "Why James Joyce Was Accepted." *Studies in the Literary Imagination* 25, no. 2 (1992): 23–30.

Detweiler, Jane. "A Piano in the Margin: Gertrude Stein 'Detected' in *Blood on the Dining-Room Floor.*" *Kentucky Philological Review* 7 (1992): 12–16.

Diaz-Diocaretz, Myriam. "Seven Aspects of Steinese." In *Avant Garde 4: Femmes=Frauen=Women,* 1990.

Dubnick, Randa K. "Two Types of Obscurity in the Works of Gertrude Stein." *Emporia State Research Studies* 24, no. 3 (1976): 5–27.

Dunlap, David. "For New York's Parks, First Statues of Famous American Women." *New York Times,* 16 July 1992, B1.

Dydo, Ulla E. "To Have the Winning Language: Texts and Contexts of Gertrude Stein." In *Coming to Light: American Women Poets in the Twentieth Century,* ed. Diane Wood Middlebrook and Marilyn Yalom. Ann Arbor: University of Michigan Press, 1985.

————. "Landscape Is Not Grammar: Gertrude Stein in 1928." *Raritan* 7, no. 1 (1987): 97–113.

Eastman, Max. "The Cult of Unintelligibility." In *The Literary Mind: Its Place in an Age of Science.* New York: C. Scribner's Sons, 1931.

Engelbrecht, Penelope. " 'Lifting Belly is a Language': The Postmodern Lesbian Subject." *Feminist Studies* 16, no. 1 (1990): 85–114.

Fifer, Elizabeth. "Put Language in the Waist: Stein's Critique of Women in Geography and Plays." *University of Michigan Papers in Women's Studies* 2, no. 1 (1975): 96–102.

————. "Is Flesh Advisable? The Interior Theatre of Gertrude Stein." *Signs* 4, no. 3 (1979) : 472–83.

————. "Rescued Readings: Characteristic Deformation in the Language of Stein's Plays." *Texas Studies in Literature and Language* 24, no. 4 (1982): 394–428.

————. " 'In Conversation': Gertrude Stein's Speaker, Message, and Receiver in *Painted Lace and Other Pieces*." *Modern Fiction Studies* 42, no. 3(1996): 465–80.

Gallup, Donald. "Always Gtrde Stein." *Southwest Review* 34 (Summer 1949): 254–58.

————. "Sound and Sense in 'Four Saints in Three Acts.' " *Bucknell Review* 5, no. 1 (1954): 1–11.

Gass, W. H. "Gertrude Stein: Her Escape from Protective Language." *Accent* 18 (Autumn 1958): 233–44.

————. "Gertrude Stein and the Geography of the Sentence." In *The World within the Word*. New York: Knopf, 1978.

————. "And: A Meditation on the Most Familiar Connective." *Harpers*, February 1984, 54–61.

"Gertie and the G.I.'s." *Time*, 16 April 1945, 26–27.

"Gertrude Stein: Her Words 'Do Get Under Their Skin.' " *Newsweek*, 27 October 1934, 24.

Goebel, Bruce. " 'If Nobody Had to Die': The Problem of Mortality in Gertrude Stein's *The Geographical History of America*." *Philological Quarterly* 70, no. 2 (1991): 237–52.

Gubar, Susan. "Blessings in Disguise: Cross-Dressing and Re-Dressing for Female Modernists." *Massachusetts Review* 22, no. 4 (1981): 477–508.

Grosser, Maurice. "Visiting Gertrude Stein." *New York Review of Books*, 6 November 1986, 36–38.

Haines, George. "Gertrude Stein and Composition." *Sewanee Review* 57, no. 3 (1949): 411–24.

Hejinian, Lyn. "Two Stein Talks: (1) Language and Realism, (2) Grammar and Landscape." *Temblor* 3 (1986): 128–39.

Hoffeld, Laura. "Gertrude Stein's Unmentionables." *The Lion and the Unicorn: A Critical Journal of Children's Literature* 2, no. 1 (1978): 48–55.

Holland, Jeanne. "Uncovering Woman's Body in Gertrude Stein's 'Subject-Cases: The Background of a Detective Story.' " *College English* 52, no. 5 (1990): 540–51.

Hubert, Renee Riese. "Gertrude Stein, Cubism, and the Postmodern Book." *Genre* 20, no. 3–4 (1987): 329–58.

Hutchison, Beth. "Gertrude Stein's Film Scenarios." *Literature/Film Quarterly* 17, no. 1 (1989): 35–38.

Johnston, Judith L. "After the Invention of the Gramophone: Hearing the Woman in Stein's *Autobiography* and Woolf's *Three Guineas*." In *Virginia Woolf Miscellanies: Proceedings of the First Annual Conference on Virginia Woolf*, ed. Mark Hussey and Vara Neverow-Turk. New York: Pace University Press, 1992.

Keith, Philip "How to Write Like Gertrude Stein." In *Audits of Meaning*, ed. Louise K. Smith. Portsmouth, N. H.: Boynton/Cook, 1988.

Kellner, Bruce. "Baby Woojums in Iowa." *Books-at-Iowa* 26 (1977): 3–18.

Knight, Christopher. "Gertrude Stein's 'Melanctha' and Radical Heterosexuality." *Studies in Short Fiction* 25, no. 3 (1988): 295–300.

Koestenbaum, Wayne. "Stein Is Nice." *Parnassus* 20 (1995): 297–319.

Kostelanetz, Richard. "Gertrude Stein: The New Literature." *The Hollins Critic* 12, no. 3 (1975): 1–15.

———. "Gertrude Stein: What She Did." *Helicon Nine: A Journal of Women's Arts and Letters* 5 (Fall 1981): 6–21.

Lachman, Arthur. "Gertrude Stein as I Knew Her: Reminiscences of Miss Stein while She Was at Radcliffe." Typescript. Gertrude Stein Papers. The Yale Collection of American Literature. Beinecke Rare Book and Manuscript Library. Yale University, New Haven, Conn.

Landon, Brooks. " 'Not Solve It But Be In It': Gertrude Stein's Detective Stories and the Mystery of Creativity." *American Literature* 53, no. 3 (1981): 487–98.

Laughlin, James. "About Gertrude Stein." *Yale Review* 77, no. 4 (1988): 528–36.

Lord, James. "Where the Pictures Were: A Memoir." *Prose* 7 (Fall 1973): 133–87.

Marcet, Jean. " 'This Must Not Be Put In A Book': Les Strategies Erotiques dans L'ecriture de Gertrude Stein." *Revue Francaise d'Etudes Americaines* 9, no. 20 (1984): 209–28.

Meyer, Steven. "Gertrude Stein Shipwrecked in Bohemia: Making Ends Meet in the *Autobiography* and After." *Southwest Review* 77, no. 1 (1992): 12–33.

Mizejewski, Linda. "Gertrude Stein: The Pattern Moves, the Woman behind Shakes It." *Women's Studies* 13, no. 1–2 (1986): 33–47.

Mobilio, Albert. "The Lost Generator: Gertrude Stein Builds a Better Reader." *Voice Literary Supplement* 69 (November 1988): 7–13.

Mossberg, Barbara. "A Rose in Context: The Daughter Construct." In *Historical Studies and Literary Criticism*, ed. Jerome J. McGann. Madison: University of Wisconsin Press, 1985.

Nichol, bp. "Gertrude Stein's Theories of Personality." *White Pelican: A Quarterly Review of the Arts* 3, no. 4 (1973): 15–23.

Perloff, Marjorie. "Poetry as Word-System: The Art of Gertrude Stein." In *The Poetics of Indeterminacy: Rimbaud to Cage*. Princeton, N.J.: Princeton University Press, 1981.

Pondrom, Cyrena. "Gertrude Stein: From Outlaw to Classic." *Contemporary Literature* 27, no. 1 (1986): 98–114.

Robinson, Marc. "No Stein Unturned." *Village Voice*, 2 April 1991.

Rohr, Susanne. " 'Everybody sees, and everybody says they do': Another Guess at Gertrude Stein's *Blood on the Dining-Room Floor*." *Amerikastudien* 41, no. 4 (1996): 593–602.

Ruddick, Lisa. "Fluid Symbols in American Modernism: William James, Gertrude Stein, George Santayana, and Wallace Stevens." In *Allegory,*

Myth, and Symbol, ed. Morton W. Bloomfield. Harvard English Studies, vol. 9. Cambridge, Mass.: Harvard University Press, 1981.

———. "William James and the Modernism of Gertrude Stein." In *Modernism Reconsidered,* ed. Robert Kiely. Harvard English Studies, vol. 11. Cambridge, Mass.: Harvard University Press, 1983.

———. "Stein and Cultural Criticism in the Nineties." *Modern Fiction Studies* 42, no. 3 (1996): 647–60.

Rust, Martha Dana. "Stop the World, I Want to Get Off: Identity and Circularity in Gertrude Stein's 'The World Is Round.'" *Style* 30, no. 1 (1996): 130–42.

Saldivar-Hull, Sonia. "Wrestling Your Ally: Stein, Racism, and Feminist Critical Practice." In *Women's Writing in Exile,* ed. Mary Lynn Broe and Angela Ingram. Chapel Hill: University of North Carolina Press, 1989.

Schmitz, Neil. "Gertrude Stein as Post-Modernist: The Rhetoric of Tender Buttons." *Journal of Modern Literature* 3, no. 5 (1974): 1203–18.

———. "A Gertrude Stein Reader." *Queen's Quarterly* 89, no. 1 (1982): 15–80.

———. "Doing the Fathers: Gertrude Stein on U. S. Grant in *Four in America.*" *American Literature* 65, no. 4 (1993):751–60.

Schultz, Susan. "Gertrude Stein's Self-Advertisement." *Raritan* 12, no. 2 (1992): 71–87.

Secor, Cynthia. "The Question of Gertrude Stein." In *American Novelists Revisited: Essays in Feminist Criticism,* ed. Fritz Fleischmann. New York: G. K. Hall, 1982.

Severijnen, Olav. "The Renaissance of a Genre: Autobiography and Modernism." *New Compassion* 9 (Spring 1990): 41–59.

Shaw, Barnett. "Encounter with Gertrude Stein." *Texas Quarterly* 9, no. 3 (1966): 21–23.

Skinner, B. F., "Has Gertrude Stein a Secret?" *Atlantic Monthly,* January 1934, 50–57.

Stewart, Lawrence. "Gertrude Stein and the Vital Dead." *Mystery and Detection Annual* 1 (1972): 102–23.

Stimpson, Catharine. "Alice and Gertrude and Others." *Prairie Schooner* 54, no. 4 (1971–72): 284–99.

———. "The Mind, the Body, and Gertrude Stein." *Critical Inquiry* 3, no. 3 (1977): 489–506.

———. "Reading Gertrude Stein." *Tulsa Studies in Women's Literature* 4, no. 2 (1985): 265–71.

———. "Gertrude Stein and the Transposition of Gender." In *The Poetics of Gender,* ed. Nancy K. Miller. New York: Columbia University Press, 1986.

———. "The Somagrams of Gertrude Stein." In *The Female Body in Western Civilization: Contemporary Perspectives,* ed. Susan Rubin Suleiman. Cambridge, Mass.: Harvard University Press, 1986.

———. "Gertrude Stein and the Lesbian Lie." In *American Women's Autobiography: Fea(s)ts of Memory,* ed. Margo Culley. Madison: University of Wisconsin Press, 1992.

Testimony Against Gertrude Stein. Supplement to *Transition* 23 (February 1935). Gertrude Stein Papers. The Yale Collection of American Literature. Beinecke Rare Book and Manuscript Library. Yale University, New Haven, Conn.

Vanskike, Elliott. "Seeing Everything as Flat': Landscape in Gertrude Stein's *Useful Knowledge* and *The Geographical History of America.*" *Texas Studies in Literature and Language* 35, no. 2 (1993): 151–67.

Van Vechten, Carl. "A Stein Song." In *Selected Writings of Gertrude Stein*, ed. Carl Van Vechten. New York: Vintage Books, 1962.

Watts, Linda. "Twice Upon a Time: Back Talk, Spinsters, and Re-Verse-als in Gertrude Stein's *The World Is Round* (1939)." *Women and Language* 16, no. 1 (1993): 53–57.

———. " 'Can Women Have Wishes': Gender and Spiritual Narrative in Gertrude Stein's 'Lend a Hand or Four Religions' (1922)." *Journal of Feminist Studies in Religion* 10, no. 2 (1994): 49–72.

Williams, William Carlos. "The Work of Gertrude Stein." *Pagany,* no. 1 (Winter 1930): 41–46.

Critical Works: Special Periodical Issues

Modern Fiction Studies 42, no. 3 (1996). *Gertrude Stein Issue.*
Twentieth Century Literature 24, no. 1 (1978). *Gertrude Stein Issue.*
The Widening Circle (Fall 1973). *Gertrude Stein, 1874–1974: A Centennial Issue.*

Biographies

Harris, Bertha. *Gertrude Stein.* Lives of Notable Gay Men and Lesbians. New York: Chelsea House,1995.

Hobhouse, Janet. *Everybody Who Was Anybody: A Biography of Gertrude Stein.* New York: Putnam, 1975.

LaFarge, Ann. *Gertrude Stein.* New York: Chelsea House, 1988.

Mellow, James R. *Charmed Circle: Gertrude Stein and Company.* New York: Praeger , 1974.

———. "Gertrude Stein." In *Dictionary of Literary Biography.* Vol. 4, *American Writers in Paris, 1920–1939.* Detroit, Mich.: Gale Research, 1980.

Souhami, Diana. *Gertrude and Alice.* San Francisco: HarperCollins, 1992.

Wagner-Martin, Linda. *'Favored Strangers': Gertrude Stein and Her Family.* New Brunswick, N.J.: Rutgers University Press, 1995.

Wineapple, Brenda. *Sister Brother: Gertrude and Leo Stein.* New York: Putnam, 1996.

Bibliographies

"Bibliography." [Gertrude Stein]. *Transition* (February 1929). Gertrude Stein Papers. The Yale Collection of American Literature. Beinecke Rare Book and Manuscript Library. Yale University, New Haven, Conn.

Firmage, George James, comp. *A Check-List of the Published Writings of Gertrude Stein.* Amherst: University of Massachusetts, 1954.

Liston, Maureen. *Gertrude Stein: An Annotated Critical Bibliography.* Kent, Ohio: Kent State University Press, 1979.

Sawyer, Julian. *Gertrude Stein: A Bibliography.* New York: Arrow Editions, 1941.

Walker, Jayne. "Gertrude Stein." In *American Women Writers: Bibliographical Essays,* ed. Maurice Duke, Jackson R. Bryer, and M. Thomas Inge. Westport: Greenwood, 1983.

White, Ray Lewis. *Gertrude Stein and Alice B. Toklas: A Reference Guide.* Boston: G. K. Hall, 1984.

Wilson, Robert. *Gertrude Stein: A Bibliography.* New York: Phoenix Bookshop, 1974.

Other Works Consulted

Abel, Elizabeth, Marianne Hirsch, and Elizabeth Langland, eds. *The Voyage In: Fictions of Female Development.* Hanover, N.H.: University Press of New England, 1983.

Abel, Sam. "The Rabbit in Drag: Camp and Gender Construction in the American Animated Cartoon." *Journal of Popular Culture* 29, no. 3 (1995): 183–202.

Alenier, Karren L. *Bumper Cars: Gertrude Said She Took Him for a Ride.* Tempe, Ariz.: Mica Press, 1997.

Allen, Paula Gunn. *The Sacred Hoop: Recovering the Feminine in American Indian Traditions.* Boston: Beacon, 1986.

Baker, Houston. *Modernism and the Harlem Renaissance.* Chicago: University of Chicago Press, 1987.

Bambara, Toni Cade, ed. *Tales and Stories for Black Folks.* Garden City, N.Y.: Doubleday, 1971.

Barrett, Ron. "A Portrait of Gertrude Steinbrenner." *National Lampoon,* July 1982, 70–73.

Bergman, David. "Strategic Camp: The Art of Gay Rhetoric." In *Gaiety Transfigured: Gay Self-Representation in American Literature.* Madison: University of Wisconsin Press, 1991.

———. *Camp Grounds: Style and Homosexuality.* Amherst: University of Massachusetts Press, 1993.

Blessing, Jennifer. *Rrose is a Rrose is a Rrose: Gender Performance in Photography.* New York: Guggenheim Foundation, 1997.

Booth, Mark. *Camp.* New York: Quartet Books, 1983.

Selected Bibliography

Butler, Judith. *Gender Trouble: Feminism and the Subversion of Identity.* New York: Routledge, 1990.

Case, Sue-Ellen. "Toward a Butch-Femme Aesthetic." In *Making a Spectacle: Feminist Essays on Contemporary Women's Theatre,* ed. Lynda Hart. Ann Arbor: University of Michigan Press, 1989.

Chaplin, Charles. *My Autobiography.* New York: Simon and Schuster, 1964.

Clayton, Jay, ed. *Influence and Intertextuality in Literary History.* Madison: University of Wisconsin Press, 1991.

Core, Philip. *Camp: The Lie That Tells the Truth.* New York: Putnam, 1984.

Creekmur, Corey, and Alexander Doty, eds. *Out in Culture: Gay, Lesbian, and Queer Essays on Popular Culture.* Durham, N.C.: Duke University Press, 1995.

Daly, Mary. *Webster's First New Intergalactic Wickedary of the English Language.* Boston: Beacon, 1987.

Dollimore, Jonathan. *Sexual Dissidence: Augustine to Wilde, Freud to Foucault.* New York: Oxford University Press, 1991.

Doty, Alexander. *Making Things Perfectly Queer: Interpreting Mass Culture.* Minneapolis: University of Minnesota Press, 1993.

Duberman, Martin Bauml, Martha Vicinus, and George Chauncey Jr., eds. *Hidden From History: Reclaiming the Gay and Lesbian Past.* New York: New American Library, 1989.

DuPlessis, Rachel Blau. "For the Etruscans." In *The New Feminist Criticism: Essays on Women, Literature, and Theory,* ed. Elaine Showalter. New York: Pantheon Books, 1985.

———. *Writing beyond the Ending: Narrative Strategies of Twentieth-Century Women Writers.* Bloomington: Indiana University Press, 1985.

Dynes, Wayne, ed. *Encyclopedia of Homosexuality.* New York: Garland, 1990.

Easthope, Antony, and John O. Thompson, eds. *Contemporary Poetry Meets Modern Theory.* Toronto: University of Toronto Press, 1991.

Epstein, Julia, and Kristina Straub. *Body Guards: The Cultural Politics of Gender Ambiguity.* New York: Routledge, 1991.

Faderman, Lillian. *Surpassing the Love of Men: Romantic Friendship and Love between Women from the Renaissance to the Present.* New York: William Morrow, 1981.

Fetterly, Judith. *The Resisting Reader: A Feminist Approach to American Fiction.* Bloomington: Indiana University Press, 1978.

Fine, Vivian. *The Women in the Garden* (chamber opera). Shaftsbury, England: Catamount, 1977.

Flynn, Elizabeth, and Patrocinio Schweickart, eds. *Gender and Reading: Essays on Readers, Texts, and Contexts.* Baltimore, Md.: Johns Hopkins University Press, 1986.

Friedman, Ellen G., and Miriam Fuchs, eds. *Breaking the Sequence: Women's Experimental Fiction.* Princeton, N.J.: Princeton University Press, 1989.

Garber, Marjorie. *Vested Interests: Cross Dressing and Cultural Anxiety.* New York: Routledge, 1992.

Giard, Robert. *Particular Voices: Portraits of Gay and Lesbian Writers.* Cambridge, Mass.: MIT Press, 1988.

Gilbert, Sandra M., and Susan Gubar. *No Man's Land: The Place of the Woman Writer in the Twentieth Century.* New Haven, Conn.: Yale University Press, 1989.

Goodwin, Joseph. *More Man Than You'll Ever Be: Gay Folklore and Acculturation in Middle America.* Bloomington: Indiana University Press, 1989.

Gray, Nancy. *Language Unbound: On Experimental Writing by Women.* Chicago: University of Illinois Press, 1992.

Guerrilla Girls. *Confessions of the Guerrilla Girls.* New York: HarperPerennial, 1995.

Hachtman, Tom. *Gertrude's Follies.* New York: St. Martin's, 1980.

———. *Fun City.* New York: St. Martin's, 1983.

Haight, Mary Ellen. *Walks in Gertrude Stein's Paris.* Salt Lake City, Utah: Peregrine Smith Books, 1988.

Harris, Daniel. *The Rise and Fall of Gay Culture.* New York: Hyperion, 1997.

Hebdige, Dick. *Subculture: The Meaning of Style.* New York: Routledge, 1991.

Hewett, Angela. "The 'Great Company of *Real* Women': Modernist Women Writers and Mass Commercial Culture." In *Rereading Modernism: New Directions in Feminist Criticism,* ed. Lisa Rado. New York: Garland, 1994.

Hillerman, Tony, and Rosemary Herbert. *The Oxford Book of American Detective Stories.* New York: Oxford University Press, 1996.

hooks, bell. *Talking Back: Thinking Feminist, Thinking Black.* Boston: South End, 1989.

Huyssen, Andreas. *After the Great Divide: Modernism, Mass Culture, Postmodernism.* Bloomington: Indiana University Press, 1986.

Jay, Karla, and Joanne Glasgow, eds. *Lesbian Texts and Contexts: Radical Revisions.* New York: New York University Press, 1990.

Kaufmann, Michael. *Textual Bodies: Modernism, Postmodernism, and Print.* Lewisburg, Penn.: Bucknell University Press, 1994.

Kiernan, Robert. *Frivolity Unbound: Six Masters of the Camp Novel.* New York: Continuum, 1990.

Klaitch, Doris. *Woman Plus Woman: Attitudes toward Lesbianism.* New York: Simon and Schuster, 1974.

Klein, Kathleen. *The Woman Detective: Gender and Genre.* 2d ed. Urbana: University of Iowa Press, 1995.

———, ed. *Women Times Three: Writers, Detectives, Readers.* Bowling Green, Ohio: Bowling Green State University Popular Press, 1995.

Knapp, James. *Literary Modernism and the Transformation of Work.* Evanston, Ill.: Northwestern University Press, 1988.

Koestenbaum, Wayne. *Jackie Under My Skin.* New York: Plume, 1996.

La Belle, Jenijoy. *Herself Beheld: The Literature of the Looking Glass.* Ithaca, N.Y.: Cornell University Press, 1988.

Lentricchia, Frank, and Thomas McLaughlin. *Critical Terms for Literary Study.* Chicago: University of Chicago Press, 1995.

Lesser, Wendy, ed. *Hiding in Plain Sight: Essays in Criticism and Autobiography.* San Francisco: Mercury House, 1992.

Lieberman, Marcia. " 'Some Day My Prince Will Come': Female Acculturation Through the Fairy Tale." In *Gender Images: Readings for Composition,* ed. Melita Schaum and Connie Flanagan. Boston: Houghton Mifflin, 1992.

Lippard, Lucy. *Mixed Blessings: New Art for a Multicultural Society.* New York: Pantheon, 1990.

Martín, Jorge Hernández. *Readers and Labyrinths: Detective Fiction in Borges, Buston Domecq, and Eco.* New York: Garland, 1995.

McClave, Heather, ed. *Women Writers of the Short Story.* Englewood Cliffs, N.J.: Prentice-Hall, 1980.

Meyer, Moe, ed. *The Politics and Poetics of Camp.* New York: Routledge, 1994.

Michasiw, Kim. "Camp, Masculinity, Masquerade." *differences* 6, no. 2–3 (1994): 146–73.

Ohmann, Richard. *The Politics of Letters.* Middletown, Conn.: Wesleyan University Press, 1987.

Olsen, Tillie. *Silences.* New York: Delacorte, 1978.

Radstone, Susannah. *Sweet Dreams: Sexuality, Gender, and Popular Fiction.* London: Lawrence and Wishart, 1988.

Rich, Adrienne. "When We Dead Awaken: Writing as Re-Vision." *College English* 34, no. 1 (1972): 18–30.

Riddel, Joseph. *The Turning Word: American Literary Modernism and Continental Theory.* Philadelphia: University of Pennsylvania Press, 1996.

Robinson, Lillian. "Dwelling in Decencies: Radical Criticism and the Feminist Perspective." *College English* 32, no. 8 (1971): 879–89.

———. "Treason Our Text: Feminist Challenges to the Literary Canon." In *The New Feminist Criticism: Essays on Women, Literature, and Theory,* ed. Elaine Showalter. New York: Pantheon Books, 1985.

Ross, Andrew. *No Respect: Intellectuals and Popular Culture.* New York: Routledge, 1989.

Rubin, Gayle. "The Traffic in Women: Notes on the 'Political Economy' of Sex." In *Toward an Anthropology of Women,* ed. Rayna Reiter. New York: Monthly Review Press, 1975.

Schmidgall, Gary. *The Stranger Wilde: Interpreting Oscar.* New York: Dutton, 1994.

Soitos, Stephen. *The Blues Detective: A Study of African American Detective Fiction.* Amherst: University of Massachusetts Press, 1996.

Solomon, Barbara, ed. *Other Voices, Other Vistas: Short Stories from Africa, China, India, Japan, and Latin America.* New York: Mentor, 1992.

Sontag, Susan. *Against Interpretation and Other Essays.* New York: Farrar, Straus, and Giroux, 1966.

Stallybrass, Peter, and Allon White. *The Politics and Poetics of Transgression.* Ithaca, N.Y.: Cornell University Press, 1986.

Steward, Samuel. *Murder is Murder is Murder.* Boston: Alyson, 1985.

———. *The Caravaggio Shawl*. Boston: Alyson, 1989.

———. *A Pair of Roses*. New York: Juniper Phitzer Press, 1993.

Straub, Kristina. *Sexual Suspects*. Princeton, N.J.: Princeton University Press, 1992.

Strohmeyer, Sarah, and Geoff Hansen. *Barbie Unbound: A Parody of the Barbie Obsession*. Norwich, England: New Victoria Publications, 1997.

Thomson, Virgil, and Georges Hugnet. *The Cradle of Gertrude Stein or Mysteries in the Rue de Fleurus*. New York: Southern Music Publishing, 1979.

Toklas, Alice B. *The Alice B. Toklas Cookbook*. London: Folio Society, 1993.

Veblen, Thorstein. *The Theory of the Leisure Class*. New York: Dover, 1994.

Wardetzky, Kristen. "The Structure and Interpretation of Fairy Tales Composed by Children." *Journal of American Folklore* 103 (April/June 1990): 157–77.

Williams, Michael. "Mart Trips Mousetrap as French Dis Disney." *Variety*, 1 June 1992, 1, 89.

Williams, Raymond. *The Politics of Modernism: Against the New Conformists*. New York: Verso, 1989.

Wilson, Anna. "Death and the Mainstream: Lesbian Detective Fiction and the Killing of the Coming-Out Story." *Feminist Studies* 22, no. 2 (1996): 251–78.

Wolfe, Susan, and Julia Penelope, eds. *Sexual Practice, Textual Theory: Lesbian Cultural Criticism*. Cambridge: Blackwell, 1993.

Zimmerman, Bonnie. "Feminist Fiction and the Postmodern Challenge." In *Postmodern Fiction: A Bio-Bibliographical Guide*, ed. Larry McCaffery. New York: Greenwood, 1986.

———. *The Safe Sea of Women: Lesbian Fiction, 1969–1989*. Boston: Beacon, 19

Index

The Author

Linda S. Watts has published articles in such journals as *Transformations: A Resource for Curriculum Transformation and Scholarship; Women and Language; Journal of Feminist Studies in Religion; Radical Teacher: A Socialist and Feminist Journal on the Theory and Practice of Teaching; Sycamore: An Online Scholarly Journal of American Studies;* and *Radical History Review.* Her book-length study, *Rapture Untold: Gender, Mysticism, and the 'Moment of Recognition' in Writings by Gertrude Stein* appeared in 1996. Watts is professor of American Studies and director of Interdisciplinary Arts and Sciences at University of Washington, Bothell.

The Editors

Gary Scharnhorst is professor of English at the University of New Mexico, coeditor of *American Literary Realism,* and editor in alternating years of *American Literary Scholarship: An Annual.* He is the author or editor of books about Horatio Alger Jr., Charlotte Perkins Gilman, Bret Harte, Nathaniel Hawthorne, Henry David Thoreau, and Mark Twain, and he has taught in Germany on Fulbright fellowships three times (1978–1979, 1985–1986, 1993). He is also the current president of the Western Literature Association and the Pacific Northwest American Studies Association.

Eric Haralson is assistant professor of English at the State University of New York at Stony Brook. He has published articles on American and English literature in *American Literature, Nineteenth-Century Literature,* the *Arizona Quarterly, American Literary Realism,* and the *Henry James Review,* as well as in several essay collections. He is also the editor of *The Garland Encyclopedia of American Nineteenth-Century Poetry.*